INTELLIGENT LOVE

IS
CHOOSING YOUR LIFE MATE WISELY

Dr. Laurie A. Moore
Copyright 2000

Couples and Individual Sessions
www.counselingscottsvalley.us
www.DrLaurieMoore.com
831-477-7007

Couples & Individual
Coaching & Readings
www.animiracles.com
831-477-7007

Table of Contents

ACKNOWLEDGEMENTS

Thank you, Ray Torres, for being my dear SunRay, my love, and my light with each breath, each day, each sunrise, and each sunset. I honor and love you with all my heart and soul. You bring me joy and delight.

Thank you Jessie Justin Joy, my dear beloved cat, the Guru of my heart and soul. I honor and love you with all my heart and soul. You bring me joy and delight.

Thank you Lisa, Maria, and Ruah for decades of support and friendship, authentic sharing, and unyielding care through both the joyful and painful times in life.

Editor: Bob Giges
This book is distributed by The Alison Frandeen Press

ISBN: **ISBN-13: 978-1490464008**

ISBN-10: 149046400X

FOREWORD

Making a commitment to a couple-relationship deserves careful thought as well as innate love. This book gives the reader seven areas of compatibility to examine when making a relationship choice. Each area is related to a chakra.

While yearning for compatible love, I read philosophies from many periods in history as well as varied cultures. There were two camps of thought going back centuries. One camp said make a list of what you seek. Another said follow your heart. It seemed to me that a combination of both were needed.

I originally wrote the book as guidance for myself. All methodologies I encountered were helpful and illuminating. Still I needed a right-match road for my personal life-approach. I sought something honoring the mysterious grace of unexplainable feelings as equally valuable to practical choice.

Writing and using my own book worked for me. I fell in love with someone who expanded my world in many wonderful ways unknown to me before. He receive the same from me. I could give much of myself authentically while sharing new worlds that deepened my heart and soul. The blend of he and I created something fully new which has evolved fifteen years. People often asked about the vibration we shared. How could they find something as delicious for themselves? Hence I offer this book.

INTRODUCTION

Yes Virginia, there is love … but no, Virginia, love is not enough.

I receive this question from a client. I thought it was unusual but then I received the same question from another. So I share it as a basis of discussion here.

Dear Dr. Laurie,

I love my boyfriend with all my heart. I wish to marry him. He is my best friend but I'm not sexually attracted to him. Is it possible for sexual attraction to grow?

—Virginia

Dear Virginia,

Love is only one of seven necessary components in choosing a life partner. Since Shakespeare's arrival, Western movies and novels have spread the idea that love is the answer to everything. In the popular movie *Splash,* a sexy heartbroken man and an unusually intelligent yet innocently sweet mermaid meet each other. Immediately, they fall into passionate love, blessed by destiny.

They find each other because he is impelled to go to Cape Cod after being dumped by his girlfriend, although he isn't sure why. Dancing in the basement of the eloquent parlor of his subconscious, warm with a soft green rug, and decorated with frilly windows from the Victorian age is the answer. He met a mermaid another time when he was in the pit of despair. At age seven he jumped into the sea and saw her. Now they meet again. This time, however, she is granted a human body when she swims the almost drowned, despondent searcher to land. Consequently, he has no idea that she is a different species when their relationship begins.

As the story continues, passion becomes love. They learn about each other's worlds in charming and funny ways. Imagine eating dinner with a mermaid who gobbles down an entire lobster, shell and antennae included. He is surprised as they sit in a posh restaurant in New York. So are a number of onlookers. Later she says, "Sorry, but that's how we eat lobster where I come from." Her mate is constantly perplexed with her unwillingness to reveal exactly where she is from, but shortly before she must depart a scientist, blinded by his own desire for fame, squirts her legs with water, causing them to disappear and her fish tail to return.

Discovering that his lady is actually a fish does not ruin this prince's love. In the end he jumps into the sea with her. Although she tells him he can't return if he goes, she states that he will be protected. As long as he stays with her he can live underwater. The movie ends here and love wins all.

Or does it? As a psychotherapist I couldn't help but imagine the next scene. The cameras are gone but I expect a call from the sexy prince in about a week. When he realizes that he cannot see his family and his job is forever gone, when it becomes clear that he has given up the life he knows for eternal swimming and a menu of raw clams, will love conquer all? This is culture shock at its worst: no family, no friends, and he doesn't speak the language of any of the other sea dwellers. To add to his discomfort, he can no longer sleep in a bed. Nothing that he enjoys doing will be a part of his life. He can't participate in his old hobbies. He can't make a living and contribute to her well-being. He can swim underwater only when he is near her.

Long term couple-hood relationship will take you to an unraveling of false ego and shadow as you are forced to unwind every part of your assumed personality. For this reason, choosing a relationship that offers basic comforts in communication, appreciation, and compatibility to begin, is an important foundation!

When following our hearts and souls, the mystery of relationships brings us into learning we never imagined beforehand. The synchronicity of relationship takes us to mirrors of self we never would encounter alone. The karma of relationship can have us feeling we must pursue relating even when rationally it doesn't make sense! Each of our relationship experiences are valid passages in life. Our success is the experience of what we give and receive. It cannot be measured by standard concepts into which the complexity of relationship never fits!

Long term couple-hood is nourished by our attention to compatibility. When the heart and soul beckon us toward another, it is a valuable idea to be intricately honest about the aspects of the pull. If we seek long term companionship that is positive and fulfilling, it behooves us to look at a variety of compatibility keys that are in alignment with the seven chakras: practical lifestyle, passion, emotional chemistry love, communication style, perspective, and grace.

The following chapters will help you to look closely at this alignment. Is it there? In what ways? Is it not? In which ways? What compromises are worth it to you? Which compromises are not? Is a new way of looking possible?

Please do not use the following chapter as a dogma or set of rules. Run it by yourself. Take what helps. Drop the rest and ultimately do what you feel best for you! While some of the category's sub topics will be important to you, others will not. You will have unique sub categories to add that are not mentioned. The idea is to be true to your own needs as a unique being of many inner landscapes and outer callings.

Long term couple-ship will challenge some of your ideas of love. While you will give to each other in ways that are healing and fulfilling, you will both fall short in some arenas. Long term couple-ship demands that you separate your ego's idea of love from whole love. You will surrender into new modes of love as you talk about your needs and uncover different assumptions. You will find that some of what you called love is narcissism while some of what you desire is the most nourishing necessity for your unique soul. You will find compromise to be as important as maintaining what cannot be healthily adjusted.

It will be murky at times and clear at others. You will question what is real. As you play in the artistic dance of couple-hood, with willingness to grow, you will deepen into a love that is truer than initial infatuation. Sometimes struggling and sometimes celebrating, you shall find out how you change and expand for one another thus yourselves. You will find unneeded limits dissolving and other boundaries strengthening. You will become more of yourself in some ways and risk straying from your essential self in others. But the straying shall soon bring you back to a deeper knowing of life's goodness if you embrace the artistic challenge with love and priorities. This depth of interplay, a garden of life, does best in a bed of compatible nutrients from the get go!

Back to our hero in **Splash**, Virginia. He does not know what he is getting into. All of a sudden, every aspect of his self-identity is taken in love. Is he ready for life's biggest lesson: you are not anything but love? How many humans will really adapt to such a dramatic occurrence? Basically, he has lost his identity, his lifestyle, and all of his relations other than his girlfriend. Will love truly conquer all?

Love and conquer are polar opposites. This kind of love will, at least, conquer his ideas of who he is, and

worst conquer his happiness. At best he will release every aspect of attachment immediately and go into bliss. But what human has done that? Most couple-ships require gradual refinement, ongoing release, and learning of the lessons one came in to discover. Is this the beginning of a spiritual journey into unconditional love? Perhaps in the long run. As of Monday, however, I can expect to see him for an adjustment disorder at best and a major depressive disorder at worse. I predict that he will schedule my first appointment of the day. His life is gone overnight. The movie leaves this part out.

His love was based on lust, which is only one of the seven significant aspects of a healthy partnership. Although love that grows out of lust can be just as real and lasting as lust that grows out of love, you need to maintain both for a fulfilling existence. This relationship can no longer be consummated. Below the belly the mermaid has a fin. Yes, there are all kinds of sexual experiences and tantric ways to energetically make love, but let's be realistic. This relationship was highly hinged on a familiar sexual dialogue. These two are in major trouble. They are on the road to disappointment.

The mermaid and the man had what you did not, Virginia. They had passion. Those two may have lacked what you do have. You have depth of friendship in heart. But neither of you have a completely fulfilling relationship ahead because that requires both passion and love.

Sexual attraction can grow between people, yes. I am a believer in miracles and magical transformations. However, if it has not grown, and prayers or creative attempts to find this spark have not paid off, make your choices on what you do share. What you do not share will likely be your life for a long time if you marry. I hear how challenging it is to feel deep love without the passion. I feel how much you love your friend and wish to be together. I also hear that you wish for lovers compatibility in a relationship.

My thought is that you will be more fulfilled with a soul mate who is a true friend and a lover too.

What do you think is best for you? Only you can decide this.

Dr. Laurie

Chapter 1
GRACE
mystery in relationship

Don't ponder why it is that you hear your lover's whisper in your own heartbeat when he is far away. Delight in the music. Don't contemplate why it is that your lover feels your presence just because you think of her. Give thanks. Don't doubt the angelic choir that sings of your shared love, suggesting that you are a guest in a theater scripted with a divine plan. Accept the invitation.

Open your palms and catch the rose petals as they fall from the balcony. Wear your cleanest clothes. Spirit has given life to a flower. The stem has given her beauty secrets to you. Women's make-up, though pretty and artistic, will never match the silky reds and cotton-candy pinks that line the dreams of love.

Grace is the unplanned rose in the ivy that grows along the path to your front door without you remembering having planted it. You were growing daffodils. You watered them, and the water seeped through the earth back toward your walkway. Where did the rose come from? Now she feels so natural to you that you think she has always been with you. You feel she is part of you. Grace arrives in your home without ever knocking on the door.

All you need to do is leave your window open. Her scent slips subtly with the wind through the window into your bedroom, your breath, your heartbeat. She tints the air with perfume. A pink light fills your home as the afternoon approaches. Grace has her own map and schedule. She can show up when you least expect her and most need her.

Grace is the gift of Spirit. When you experience inexplicable love, when miracles occur that are beyond your ability to analyze, when you follow a path trustingly and assuredly but with no practical basis, you are responding to grace.

When have you experienced grace? When has your life felt blessed or magic? When you let your heart listen to the words of Spirit, you will know your own magic. When you are going through your day and suddenly feel the presence of your beloved in your heart, you will know your lover's magic. When you feel that a delicious play is being written and you are called to participate, you feel grace.

STORIES OF GRACE

Grace's surprises can be offered at any time in a relationship. As a relationship grows older, grace can still enter the scene like a newborn. Nicole loved and lived with her husband, Leonard, for three decades. Leonard was good to her, caring, and compassionate. While Nicole deeply appreciated him and chose to stay with him because of his warmth, she was very disappointed because he didn't engage in fun activities with her. Being a woman of numerous interests, social prowess, and love of companionship, she longed for a mate who would join her in adventure and social life. Leonard did not do this.

Leonard didn't like to leave the house. Unless he was on his way to work, he wasn't going out. This was deeply painful to Nicole, but she lived with it because she was nurtured by his care, humor, and understanding at home. By the time that Nicole proposed a move to Hawaii, he wasn't leaving the house at all. He had developed sciatica and was on disability.

Nicole and Leonard lived in a beautiful seaside town when they were first married. By the time that their kids were adults, the peaceful town had grown into a noisy city. Nicole asked Leonard to move to Hawaii with her, and he said no in the same way that he had said no about going anywhere for many years. Nicole decided that she was not willing to live an unhappy life and told Leonard that she was moving to Hawaii with or without him as soon as their sons finished graduate school. Leonard decided to go with her.

When they arrived, Leonard was in such physical pain that Nicole had to push him around in a wheelchair. For some inexplicable reason Leonard agreed to go to the ocean and let Nicole float him. He had never liked swimming before. Leonard was not a happy fellow and didn't expect to ever be so. However, the experience felt wonderful to him and he was grateful. After a month of living in Hawaii and feeling gratitude for the move, Leonard was cured of sciatica, had become a swimmer himself, became Nicole's social acolyte, and said that he was a happy person and very appreciative of where he lived.

When Nicole decided to give herself what she needed, grace gave her something she had always wanted yet learned to live without. When Leonard filled his heart with gratitude, grace surprised him beyond his expectations.

Leonard had not been happy with his wife because she was non-supportive of him. He resigned himself to an unhappy marriage in order to give his kids a two-parent home. Secretly, he thought that he would leave when the children were grown up. Meanwhile, he was consistently kind and loving to his wife and children, thankful for the kids and for his wife's loving mothering of them.

Every night, however, faced with longing and loneliness, he prayed that he would find a woman who would be a best friend to him when the timing could be better. When his kids grew up and Leonard was getting ready to tell Nicole that he was going to leave, she went through an unexpected shift and began to be supportive, loving, and kind to her husband. To Leonard's surprise, he was given the woman he had spent years praying for, and that woman was his transformed wife. He was grateful. His wife's new friendship became as consistent and dependable as her previous non-supportive treatment had been. Grace changed his life and his sorrows.

GRACE COMPATIBILITY TEST

The following test will help you determine how strong the quality of grace is in your relationship. Different personalities put more or less value on grace, but every mate-relationship requires some level of grace or the relationship feels out of place, out of union, and unappealingly flat. **Read each statement and choose the one that most closely represents you. You will score your relationship on a continuum of -2 to 2.**

-2 My true desire to be in this relationship is non-existent. Due to practical circumstances, however, I am hanging in here for now.

-1 I feel that this relationship is sheer work. I am constantly having to exercise tremendous will power. Everything has to be forced into place and never quite gets there anyway. I remain in this relationship for reasons that matter to me. Nevertheless, I feel burdened.

0 This relationship is half work and half ease.

1 This relationship comes easily. We have our misunderstandings and areas of challenge, but overall our life together works out well. I feel good about being in this relationship. I feel that life is on our side.

2 Many magical and unexplainable events have occurred in this relationship. I often feel that my relationship is a gift from Spirit. I feel blessed. I am being given experiences that I could not have previously imagined. I am drawn to my mate and to our path together by a mysterious feeling that generates great energy in me. We have our conflicts, but they are well worth working through because the core of our relationships feels like a precious gift.

Understanding Your Score

Below 0 There is an inadequate amount of grace in your relationship. This relationship will contribute to a life of ongoing difficulty.

0 This kind of life will be adequate for some but not for others, depending upon your standards. People have different expectations regarding grace. If you score 0 ask yourself, "How important is grace to me?" Some people can survive on a menu of just a little grace as an appetizer, while others find it to be the main ingredient in a diet that keeps them healthy. You will know if you are satisfied or dissatisfied with the degree of grace in your life. Trust your own judgment.

1-2 You have chosen a relationship that provides enough grace to offer you ongoing experiences of satisfaction and even ecstasy.

HOW TO DEVELOP MORE GRACE IN YOUR LIFE: GRACE IS RELATED TO GRATITUDE

Look at yourself before blaming a partner. When you are not experiencing grace in a relationship, you will benefit by looking at your personal connection to grace before making a definitive decision about staying in or leaving the relationship. In order to receive grace in a relationship you must first be tuned to grace as an individual.

Although you cannot direct grace, you can offer gratitude. There is a direct correlation between how much gratitude you give to life and others, and how often grace comes to visit you. The opportunity for gratitude exists in every moment. The more you take this opportunity, the more you will discover grace in your daily life.

One evening I was driving on an exceptionally busy street with very rude drivers. I was headed somewhere to give a talk about sexuality. Drivers were so aggressive that I was experiencing tremendous difficulty getting into the turning lane. When I missed my turn I felt irate.

Suddenly I thought of my sister, who will never be able to drive due to a physical limitation. I felt embarrassed and realized that I was extremely fortunate. Gratitude spread through my chest like the feeling of warm sun on skin after a long winter. I thanked life for giving me the opportunity to drive. I thanked life for giving me the opportunity to present lectures, to travel, and to create my own career.

Once my mind got on the gratitude track, it kept going. I was grateful to be alive, to breathe, and to be on my way to do something I love. I was astounded that my career allowed me to network with wonderful people, and that I was surrounded by friends everywhere. I was happy to live near the beach. The contrast of the heavy traffic on this street to my neighborhood magnified my gratitude for where I lived.

By the time that I arrived to give my lecture I was so happy that I forgot to be nervous and had a stupendous time. A number of people enrolled in my workshops, and I was told by the organization's president that I gave the best talk I had ever given there. My gratitude led me to receive precious gifts of life.

There is always something to be grateful about, and there is always something to complain about. When you make gratitude a way of living you will find that contentment is an optional habit. Those who practice gratitude find contentment. Those who are content notice the many ways that grace is in their lives.

EXERCISE I: CREATING MORE GRACE IN YOUR LIFE

If you carry out the following exercise every day for a month, you are very likely to experience new and unexpected moments of grace. This exercise will take your focus to your friends and associates, your body, your career, and your finances, as well as to your significant other. People who are consistently grateful in these areas tend to be happier with their mates. Dissatisfaction in any of these realms of life often spills into one's primary relationship.

You will need a journal and a pen.

Days one through six:

Each morning, spend five minutes thinking about things others have done for you for which you are grateful. For example, I am grateful to my partner for being such a good listener. I am grateful to my mother for loving me. I am grateful to my best friend for taking me out to lunch. I am grateful to my cat for being affectionate with me. Even though my colleague hurt my feelings yesterday, I am grateful that he was honest with me. Write all of your thoughts down in a journal used solely for gratitude entries.

Repeat this again in the evening.

Day seven:

Give yourself a rest from your journal writing.

Days eight through thirteen:

Spend ten minutes in the morning thinking about all of the ways in which you can be grateful for your own body. For example, I am grateful to my body for allowing me to go on wonderful walks. I am grateful to my body for being healthy most of the time. Even though I am currently experiencing a medical challenge, I am grateful to my body for giving me the pleasure of good feelings when I get a massage. I am grateful to my body for allowing me to taste delicious foods. Record all of your thoughts in your gratitude journal.

Repeat this exercise in the evening.

Day fourteen:

Give yourself a rest from your journal writing.

Days fifteen through twenty:

For fifteen minutes in the morning, focus on all the ways that you are grateful to your career and the income it provides. For example, I am grateful for money because it bought the computer that allowed me to write this book. I am thankful to my career which leads me to the readers who will benefit from this book. I am grateful for money because it allows me to rent an office so my clients and I have a warm and nourishing place to meet. I am thankful for my career because it trained me to support my clients' well-being. I am grateful for the change I found in my pocket because it allowed me to buy a brownie after lunch. Even though I have less money than most of my friends and clients, I am grateful that the money I do have allows me to host dinner parties and buy wonderful gifts for birthdays. I am grateful to my career because it allows me to earn money for something I enjoy doing. Even though I am often saddened by the painful stories I hear as a psychotherapist, I am thankful to have a role in turning those stories around.

Write down your thoughts in your gratitude journal.

Repeat this same exercise at night.

Day twenty-one:

Give yourself a rest from your journal writing.

Days twenty-two through twenty-seven:

For twenty minutes each morning and evening, focus on all the things about your mate for which you are grateful. If you don't have a mate, focus on aspects of previous relationships for which you are grateful. (People who remember the good in previous relationships tend to create more good in future relationships. People who remain resentful and blame others for past relationships tend to cause themselves more trouble in future relationships.) For example, I am grateful to my partner for playing with me in the swimming pool yesterday. I am grateful to my ex-husband for all the times that he went out dancing with me. I am grateful to my partner for giving me feedback about the book I am writing. I am grateful to my ex-partner because he often complimented me on my creative ideas. Even though my present partner is not as playful as I desire, I am grateful for the ways that he does make me smile and laugh. Keep your thoughts recorded in your gratitude journal.

It is okay to repeat the same things on your gratitude list again and again. You can be grateful for your job, your friends, your family, your life mate, your existence, and anything else every day. Gratitude fills the soul. Even if you choose to be grateful for only one thing for the rest of your life, you will benefit from that. Ultimately, it is not what life brings to you that causes your happiness. It is what you bring to life with your heart that allows you to feel fulfilled. However, the more you bring thanks to life, the more gifts life will bring to you.

EXERCISE II: CREATING MORE GRACE IN YOUR LIFE

This exercise can be done as frequently as you like. The more you practice, the better you become at it.

Sit quietly and listen to your heart. Ask for guidance about discovering the perfect mate for you. Listen, watch, and feel. You may hear voices, see pictures, or feel emotions and sensations. You may also feel energy presences. Receive what comes to you even if it doesn't yet make practical sense. The more you do this, the clearer the guidance will become. Trust the guidance.

To differentiate between guidance and your own will, begin to notice the messages that come in a very light and energizing way. The messages that fill you with positivity and energy—whether they come in visual, auditory, somatic, emotional, or energetic form—are the messages to follow.

Relationships With and Without Grace

Couples who have no grace in their relationships will feel dry, empty, and bored. When Ruth was in a relationship with little grace she frequently tried to make the relationship feel good. She had to work hard and constantly try new approaches because there was little magic between the two people. She even resorted to drinking coffee and eating chocolate to feel good, which she had been able to do naturally before.

Ruth said, "Mitch, my boyfriend, broke up with me because he said that my life was a constant affirmation, He told me that I didn't need to work so hard and that I was making it clear that he wasn't the guy for me.

"As soon as it ended, the feeling of grace in life came back to me after seven months of feeling depleted and half dead. My creative urge, enthusiasm for adventure, and excitement about life returned almost immediately. Where had it gone? My sexual energy came back full force. I had lost it soon after the relationship began and attributed the loss to the negative effects of a new type of hormonal birth control I was trying out. Soon after that I fell deeply in love, and I didn't have to work or try or come up with ways to feel the magic of being in love. No affirmations were necessary. I could count on myself and my partner, but equally important, I could count on the powers that be to guide, carry and take care of us. Something beyond my will brought my partner and me together, and there was great relief in this. This did not guarantee that it would last forever, but it allowed me to feel happy for the first time in my life that if it did I would have a wonderful time with it."

When you are in a relationship that contains grace, magic surrounds you with ease and little effort. To keep the grace alive you simply enjoy, communicate, and be thankful. Couples who are graced will find that they feel a sense of magic and wonder. When grace is present, conflict approached healthily will lead to deeper states of intimacy and honeymoon feelings. Conflict approached in a healthy manner when grace is absent may lead to mental clarity, but it will not remove the boredom and the feeling that you are lacking something vital.

GRACE IS A GIFT IN SURRENDER

While gratitude opens the door for grace, it cannot determine what type of grace you are given. In other words, your ability to be thankful will bring you more to be thankful about. However, life's gifts may not come in the packages you request. If you ask for love, don't assume that the best love for you will come in the package you preconceive.

To be with your ideal mate you must ask for guidance from deep within. As long as you try to control what happens, you will not find what you seek. For years I made lists of the perfect mate for me. Each time I made a list, the person I desired appeared and ultimately caused me anguish, so I refined the list and started over. When I finally abandoned the list project and asked the universe to bring me a man who had a habit of making me happy all of the time just by being himself and vice versa, he appeared. This took incredible faith in Spirit. I had to go through a lot of pain before I decided to trust Spirit more than myself. By this time I was also clear about what I needed in terms of the eight basic categories, but I was willing to let go of any preconceived details. I had gone through so much heartbreak that I felt I needed to trust something greater than my own will power—either that or become a cynic. Faith worked. Faith is another component of being receptive to grace.

Life brings you to another person for reasons you cannot understand, until you shed your make-up and walk upon the path next to the rose. The man who has lost touch with his wild nature and the woman who needs to be bedded safely find each other. Like jasmine vines intertwining in the tender gardener's trellis, he and she are mysteriously pulled to each other. They drink of the sweet-scented rain water that has splashed onto each other's petals. Are you this man or this woman?

Grace gives her gifts in a climate of trust and surrender. Wise as an elder, grace answers the questions you ask with your heart before your head can recognize what is happening. When grace wants to touch you she sends her messenger, Mystery. Mystery alluringly circles around you in ways that the intellect cannot explain. Mystery rests her head in the lap of grace. Grace knows.

Chapter 2
Perspective
wisdom in relationship

Perspective is made of the candlelight with which you warm your thoughts, the stories with which you rinse your hands, and the perceptions that turn plain flour into sweet delights for dessert. You trade perspective as frequently as you trade money. You feel anxious so you call a friend for a fresh viewpoint. You suspect that there is a more efficient way to accomplish your task, so you go to the library or the Internet for information. You want to get out of a rut or shed old mental habits, so you go to another country where you are able to visit life through another culture's perspective.

The way that you experience life is shaped by the way that you perceive life. You will see life through different perspectives as you grow, change, and encounter new situations. You will find that you have a tendency to see life in particular ways, as do those around you. You will also find that you can change your way of seeing at any time, as can your partner, friends, family, and colleagues.

Who influences the way you perceive life the most? The answer is those with whom you spend the most time: your mate, your children, your family, your friends, your colleagues, and the media. Certainly you want to choose a mate whose perspective contributes to your life in a positive way.

Perspective is related to the chakra of wisdom, located on the forehead between the eyes and sometimes referred to as the "third eye."

DO I HAVE THE RIGHT TYPE OF PERSPECTIVE IN MY RELATIONSHIP?

Ever have a challenging day at work and tell your significant other about it, only to end up feeling worse? Ever come home from a horrible day, unload on your mate, and end up feeling wonderful? Your mate's use of perspective will affect your experience of living as much as you affect your own experience of living. Certain types of perspective will be favorable to you, while others will not suit you.

Diana had an excruciating day when she was informed that there would be an unexpected meeting in her department at the high school, and that she would be leading it because the regular chairperson was sick. Diana had high standards and preferred to prepare methodically for events. Being told at 5 p.m. that she would be leading a meeting at 8 a.m. the next morning was upsetting to her. She was not given ample time to do as good a planning job as she would have liked.

Diana shared this information with her boyfriend Ed over the dinner table. Ed said, "Sounds like they don't like you at work. Maybe they want to fire you."

Ed's reaction came from left field, made no sense, did not help, and introduced a new fear. This type of response was common for Ed. His perspective did not support Diana's well-being. Instead, his perspective caused her unnecessary added stress. Ed often came up with left-field, non-supportive statements. After five months, Diana ended the relationship as a result of this.

When choosing a mate, it is important that his or her perspective supports and contributes to you. A benefit of having a mate's perspective is that a mate can inspire, educate, and alter your perceptions in a valuable way, one that is different from what you can offer yourself.

Tek came home infuriated with his boss. "He uses me. He doesn't respect me. You wouldn't believe what he did today!" Tek shared a lengthy twenty-minute synopsis about all the horrible things that his boss had done. He took a big breath of air and began to look relieved, but minutes later he began to upset himself again by repeating parts of the story.

Sheila gently put her hands on his shoulders, looked him in the eyes, and said, "Tek, your boss was very unfair to you and I am so sorry about that. Now, I want to hear about you instead of your boss. What can I do to help you have a good evening and feel better?"

Tek was grateful to his wife. She was wise enough to know that he needed to vent, but when the catharsis became indulgent escalation, she stopped him and refocused him to look for a solution, rather than obsessing over the problem. She helped him to redirect his attention from the problem to a solution.

Different people prosper from different types of perspectives. Some people like to hear new perceptions and analyses of interesting events. Some people like to learn how to do things better. Some like the simple perspective of care that Sheila offered to Tek. Most people like varied types of perspectives. It is important to choose a mate whose perspective is valuable to you.

People will move through different perspectives at various times in their lives. Most people use each of the perspectives of the personality types defined below at some time or another. Nobody is truly one personality type only. However, people will tend toward utilizing one or several predominant personality types. Rather than using the types to fit people into unchangeable positions in your mind, use them to help identify what does and doesn't work for you. This way you improve your ability to ask for what you want, giving to another from an expanded repertoire of choices, and also choosing a mate that suits you well much of the time.

Chamelia was one of the best coaches in the valley. She had helped countless people turn their lives around. Her greatest asset was her perspective. No matter what problem a client presented, Chamelia could offer a new and very positive perspective on the situation. Chamelia had encountered great struggle and great joy in her life. She had a knack for turning problems into solutions. Most of her clients attributed her talent to her ability to see things in a new light. She developed this skill because this is what she needed to do in order to address the many troubles she encountered in her own history.

Chamelia dated Austin, a contractor. Every time Austin encountered a problem with his crew he would tell Chamelia and she would offer a new way for him to look at his situation. Austin and Chamelia came to therapy with me because Austin said that Chamelia was pushy.

Austin didn't know what he wanted from Chamelia, but he knew what he didn't want. He didn't want her advice. By answering a number of questions he came to realize that he really wanted sympathy. He wanted his girlfriend to say, "Oh honey, I'm sorry you had a hard day." When Chamelia was upset he gave her sympathy. She didn't do the same for him. He was feeling uncared for.

Chamelia explained that she didn't like to give sympathy. She valued solutions. Having experienced many challenges in her life, she had adopted a warrior spirit. To her, sympathy encouraged a feeling of powerlessness.

When asked why he was with Chamelia, Austin explained that they both had high income levels, both liked to travel to the same types of places, both liked to decorate their home similarly, and both liked to go out dancing on weekends. They liked the same kind of music, were both happy living as a couple without children, and had the same religious practice. They found each other to be very attractive, but all of the advice-giving was lessening Chamelia's magnetism in Austin's experience. Austin had made his choice based upon practical life and passion, but his needs for perspective and well-being were not being met.

This scenario differs from the case of Tek, who experienced his wife Sheila's perspective as a contribution. Chamelia's perspective was constructive and could have been valuable to someone who desired a new perspective. However, it was not the kind of perspective that Austin desired. Consequently, both members of the duo felt disappointed. Austin was not getting a perspective that furthered his happiness. Chamelia was offering her perspective and it was not being valued. It is mandatory that you choose a mate who respects, values, honors, and prospers from your perspective. Equally important is choosing a mate who has a perspective that benefits you.

Chamelia and Austin were able to find a more satisfying way to remain together by expanding their perspectives. Austin showed Chamelia that sympathy was a helpful response that didn't disempower him. He pointed out that when he gave sympathy to her, Chamelia felt cared for and able to move forward with a solution. Chamelia agreed to practice being sympathetic. She discovered to her surprise that Austin bounced back from his troubles much more quickly when she did.

It is important to get your perspective needs met in a relationship, so if you are looking for a partner you will want to choose one who either already offers a perspective that delights you, or has enough flexibility to realize what pleases you and learn to offer it. If you are already in a relationship and dissatisfied with your mate's perspective, see if he or she would be willing to experiment with new approaches. Chamelia found that her identity was not dismantled by trying on another style. Instead, her repertoire of life responses grew and, consequently, so did her ease in life. Not only could she speak to others with more options, but her inner dialogue with herself became more versatile. Increasing your range of perspectives will benefit you as well as a partner who has encouraged you to make this change.

PERSPECTIVE COMPATIBILITY TEST

The following test will assist you in determining how compatible you are with your potential mate in the area of perspective. Read each statement and choose the one that most closely represents you. Score your relationship on a continuum of -2 to 2.

-2 One or both of the following statements is/are true:

My mate's perspective makes me feel unhappy.

My perspective makes my mate feel unhappy.

-1 One or both of the following is/are true:

My mate's perspective is irrelevant to me.

My perspective is irrelevant to my mate.

0 Sometimes our perspectives benefit each other, and other times they don't.

1 Both of us are happy with each other's perspective.

2 In general, both my mate and I experience each other's perspective as a contribution to the quality of our lives, and we are deeply grateful for each other's perspective.

Understanding Your Score

Below 0 There is a lack of contributing perspective in your relationship. This relationship will not be happy unless both partners work on varying their perspective. If you are in the pre-committed phase of relationship and a change is not made to your satisfaction, consider finding someone with whom you share more compatible perspectives.

0 You can do better. This relationship will benefit by each of you working on adding more options to your perspective. If you are in the pre-committed phase of relationship and a change is not made to your satisfaction, consider finding someone with whom you share more compatible perspectives. Do you want your life to be okay or wonderful?

1-2 You are with someone who is a good partner for you in the area of perspective. This part of your life will bring you satisfaction and delight.

THE TEN PERSPECTIVE PERSONALITY TYPES

If you are unhappy with your mate's perspective and don't know why, it will help you to think about different kinds of perspective personality types. When you wish to get a new outfit for a party but don't have a specific one in mind, you might flip through a catalog or visit a store. Whether an outfit or a relationship is on your mind, if you don't know what you want and you don't like what you have, it will benefit you to gain clarity about what you seek. It is necessary to have a sense of what is out there in order to know what is right for you. Following are some different types of perspective that you will repeatedly find in the world.

Positive Perspective

Any life story can become a source of value if seen with a positive perspective. With a positive perspective you can see the good in life regardless of the fleeting circumstances.

Tony was afraid that he was not going to pass his accounting exam. Cheryl said, "Tony, I know how smart you are. You can do anything you set your mind to. More importantly, you are a very special man. All the people who love you will continue to love you if you fail the exam and pass it later on another try. You have a lot to be proud about whether you do or don't pass this exam first time around."

Cheryl was able to turn Tony's situation into a win regardless of how it played out. She was also able to see him in a good light when he was experiencing self-doubt. She maintained her faith in his ability when he was fearful. Her positive perspective made him feel that he was worthy, loved, and capable. It also helped him to pass his exam the first time around.

Educational Perspective

Although an educational perspective is also positive, it is more than that. An educational perspective offers new insight and awareness. Someone with an educational perspective will draw connections and lessons from situations, thereby enriching life and making the most out of everything. After going to the art gallery, Gregory discussed his observations of local artist Bonnie Park's paintings in great depth. He wondered about the color use. He commented on how her use of shadow affected his moods. He was curious about how much of her painting process was spontaneous and what was calculated.

Gregory's partner Terry loved to hear him speak. "Without Gregory I would never think about these things. After a party I would simply clean up and go to sleep. Gregory has made my life so much more interesting with his thought process. That's one of my favorite things about him."

Supportive Perspective

Someone with this perspective listens from the heart and responds to what you are needing rather than to what you are saying intellectually. While this type of perspective is supportive like a positive perspective, there is a difference. This perspective is used to read between the lines. While a positive perspective leads someone to respond supportively to what you have said, a supportive perspective means they will respond supportively to what you haven't said as well.

Joanne screamed, "My employees are impossible!"

Kurt gave her a long hug.

Joanne said, "My first husband would have asked me a million questions and tried to solve the problem, but Kurt always knows exactly what I really need."

Pure Perspective

A person who sees life through a pure perspective gets to the essence of the situation immediately. She dives down to catch the pearl, the purpose, and the answer. She doesn't swim around in the seaweed of details. You can benefit from the clear water that ripples from her opinions. This perspective is a way of synthesizing what you are saying into the simplest and cleanest form. A person using a pure perspective differs from a person using a supportive perspective because he or she is paying attention to the details of the intellect. A supportive perspective originates in the heart. A pure perspective originates in the mind. Both, of course, are equally valuable and valid. Which one suits you best is a matter of individual preference.

Bonnie said, "We can't travel together because we don't get along at all. First you say you want to go swimming, and then when we get our suits on and walk outside you change your mind. Then you say you want to go to a restaurant, but when we arrive at the Thai House you look unhappy. On the airplane you said you might want earphones, but I paid for them and you didn't use them. We have so many different troubles that we should cancel the trip we planned for next spring."

Darryl said, "Bonnie, all of the troubles you listed sound essentially the same. My frequent change of mind burdens you. I will practice sticking to my decisions if you will practice being patient with me."

Bonnie went from feeling overwhelmed with numerous problems to feeling excited about their trip. The source of their troubles now appeared to be quite manageable, thanks to Darryl's pure perspective and willingness to change.

"Life is Good" Perspective
A person who rides the weeks of life through a "life is good" perspective is here to live life to the fullest. She's not interested in creating conflict. Her basic attitude is that there is no problem worth ruining a good day. A person using this perspective will be as positive as someone using a positive perspective. The difference is that a person with a positive perspective is focused on giving you support, while a person with a "life is good" perspective is focused on creating joy. The positive perspective is used by an archetypal nurse. The "life is good" perspective is used by someone who likes to share pleasure.

Benjamin had a habit of focusing on the negative. "I'm going to stay in bed today. That argument we had last week is on my mind again. Work has been awful. I don't even want to get up."

"Let's go swimming, sweetheart," Martine responded. "It's a beautiful day and that argument was over days ago."

Benjamin got up to go and felt happy. He later explained, "My ex-girlfriend got really involved in my problems, and I used to get more depressed talking to her. She had good intentions, but her personality was so much like mine that we dragged each other down a hole. I know I can be overly negative. Martine is naturally cheery and pulls me out of my melancholy nature. This is what I love. She's the best!"

Inquisitive Perspective

When someone uses an inquisitive perspective, he or she is focusing on getting clear information, similar to someone using a pure perspective. This approach differs, however, because one gains clarity through questions rather than distillation and purification. A person who approaches life with an inquisitive perspective never jumps to conclusions. Instead, she asks you many questions, inviting you to openheartedly greet the opportunity to look at things from a variety of angles.

Bruce said, "Let's paint the house light blue. The light blue paint is on sale."

Carol asked, "What kind of mood do you think light blue will create? How long do you think it will be before the light blue walls get dirty? Do you like the light blue as much as the ocean blue? How long is the sale? Will the ocean blue be on sale any time in the near future?"

Bruce enjoyed Carol's questions. Bruce often picked the least expensive and quickest route when making a decision. Carol's perspective invited him to make decisions that took more of his needs into account. "Thanks to Carol, we have made a lot of decisions that left us happier in the long run. Carol's way of thinking is of great value in my life."

Inclusive Perspective

A person who moves through life with an inclusive perspective is aware that there are as many stories involved in a situation as there are people. Like those who use inquisitive perspectives, the person with an inclusive perspective has as many questions as answers. He differs, however, in that his main goal is to make sure that everyone is treated with compassion and respect. His main value is inclusion. A person who uses an inquisitive perspective, on the other hand, values information. You could say that a person with an inquisitive perspective is a philosopher, while a person who draws upon an inclusive perspective is an archetypal parent. This person helps others to develop compassion for everyone involved. This person is a good mediator. He will remind you to hold others in the arms of positive regard.

Lucy complained to Richard that "our twins are being selfish again."

"What did Steph and Deb do?" he asked.

"They forgot to do their chores again."

"Let's check in with them and see what was going on, Lucy."

"Sure."

After talking to the twins their parents learned that Steph had promised their neighbor, Jarvis, that she would help him with a fund-raising project. When she discovered that she had taken on more than she anticipated, Steph asked Deb to help. Both of the girls lost track of the time and didn't get to their own chores. It turned out that the girls hadn't been selfish at all.

Having taken the time to inquire and talk, the family could now come up with a constructive solution. From now on chores would have to be done before going out to play, doing a project, helping a friend, or anything else. This time, however, since the promise to Jarvis was already set in motion, Richard and Lucy would help with the fund-raising project for a couple of hours so that the girls could catch up on their chores.

Lucy was thankful to Richard for guiding her away from jumping to an inaccurate conclusion.

Solution-Oriented Perspective

A person who focuses on life with a solution-oriented perspective looks for the solution to any difficulty. In this person's mind the problem is simply an indicator that something better is available, and he will figure out what that is and how to create it. Like people who use all of the other perspectives mentioned above, someone using this perspective intends to create a positive outcome. What is unique about this perspective is that someone using it will value a positive outcome over anything else. Reaching this positive outcome is more important than pleasure, support, or empathy. These are all tools. The outcome is the priority when one uses this perspective. You will find that a person with this perspective responds to your concerns with constructive action.

James said, "Jeannie, we don't make love the way we used to. What's up with you? Things are going downhill."

Jeannie seduced him.

Jeannie said a week later, "James, you don't help around the house enough. What's your problem?"

James picked up the vacuum cleaner. Both members of this relationship could have become defensive and responded to the attack argumentatively. Instead, each opted to make life work immediately with a solution.

Empathetic Perspective

A person with this type of perspective will put her heart and mind into your situation. Similar to someone utilizing a supportive perspective, this person has deep empathy. But he or she is focused on valuing, receiving, and understanding your experience, whereas the user of a supportive perspective is focused on comforting. The person using an empathetic perspective is an archetypal witness of feelings. This kind of person offers deep compassion and understanding for others' experiences.

Leslie was very excited about an invitation to a party. She was an extrovert and loved to socialize. David had a challenging week and wanted to stay home. When Leslie shared her excitement about the party, David was immediately excited for her. David's own desires and needs didn't impede his ability to feel his partner's joy. She loved this about him. Regardless of what David was experiencing, Leslie knew that he could simultaneously empathize with her experience. This gave her a sense of being understood and cared about.

Accepting Perspective

A person who offers an accepting perspective is good at listening. He or she is an archetypal witness of words. Like the person who uses a solution-oriented perspective, this person listens with an intention of you having the best. The priority, however, is simply to hear and validate what you have said. This person wants to hear what you have to say. This person will not try to fix, change, or rearrange what you have to share. He or she is a benign witness.

When Julie came home from work she enjoyed telling Arthur about her adventures. Julie was a graphic designer who often got to meet with other graphic designers and attend seminars in New York City. She loved to tell Arthur all about the people she met, the designs she saw, and the new skills she acquired. Arthur loved to listen. Arthur was fulfilled by hearing Julie's interesting stories. He was a perfect audience for her, which delighted her because she liked to be heard.

Playful Perspective

This perspective is similar to a "life-is-good" perspective in that the person using it enjoys pleasure. He or she turns life into a fun event, approaching situations like improvisational games. The main concern is having fun in the moment.

Kai was irritated at Sam because he forgot to take out the garbage. It was one of his jobs, and the garbage truck came and left. "I'm pissed!" Kai said. Sam apologized and then tickled her. He pretended to be someone who was surrounded with garbage and never took it out. His playful nature appealed to Kai, who joined in on the improvisation. She exaggerated her angry feelings, becoming a character who was very mean, but she did it in a dramatic and playful way. She and her husband were both aware that she was having fun and venting in a way that was not abrasive to Sam. Kai was often in awe of Sam because he could turn any event into something fun.

Humorous Perspective

Someone who uses this perspective draws upon the wisdom and nature of children, just like someone who uses a playful perspective. He or she aims to bring people to laughter with their style of antics. Both of these perspectives take people far away from their dissatisfaction and straight into the here and now. The playful perspective does this with interaction. The humorous perspective does this with wit and laughter.

Carlos was depressed after hearing that he was not getting promoted. Peyton told him a joke. Carlos laughed himself back to a state of joy. Carlos cherished and admired Peyton. Nobody else could cut through his sad moments in a quick instant like she did.

CAUTIOUN OF DEGENERATIVE PERSPECTIVES

A number of other perspectives encountered in the world are at best unhelpful and at worst damaging to a mate. If you are dating someone with one of the following perspectives, you will benefit by leaving the relationship. If you have one of these perspectives, you will benefit yourself and your partner by changing it.

Each of the perspectives is available to anyone at any time. Nothing forces you to use only one perspective. If you are not serving yourself or those around you with your perspective, you may want to try one of the other ones mentioned. Try a few. Try them all. Try different ones at different times. Try a playful perspective and make it into a game if you like.

I have a trait of expressing whatever is happening in my life in a dramatic way. I can be very sad one minute and happy ten minutes later. While I enjoy feeling life to the fullest but not hanging on to any emotion, I often confuse people. "How can you be so happy if you were so sad ten minutes ago?" people often ask.

"I can be happy because I allowed myself to feel my sadness fully so it passed quickly," I say.

My ex-boyfriend Mark naturally uses a supportive perspective. When we first got together he took my disappointments and frustrations very seriously. Because I expressed them often, he thought that I was having an extraordinarily hard life. He came to realize that I was expressing whatever happened to me, and that whenever it was sad or frustrating, it was followed by happiness soon thereafter. He decided that when I was sad, he would simply witness the sadness rather than ask numerous questions. This way I bounced back into joy easily and quickly. When he asked numerous questions I became sadder and sadder because all my energy went toward focusing on the sorrow rather than feeling it and moving on. Although he was excellent at utilizing both a supportive and inquisitive perspective, which were of great use in his career, Mark discovered that an empathetic perspective was more valuable to me. I still appreciate him deeply for that.

DEGENERATIVE PERSPECTIVE TYPES
For every healthy perspective there is a corresponding unhealthy perspective.

Negative Perspective
When someone is drawing upon this type of perspective, he will look at most situations as though something unfavorable has occurred. He will find the worst in everything. When you are in a conversation with someone

who maintains a negative perspective, you are likely to feel that you are being pulled into a well of hot, sticky tar.

Falsely Educational Perspective

When someone looks at life through this perspective she enjoys being the teacher without regard for what she is imparting. In fact, she may even fabricate things for the sake of receiving another's attention. A person using this perspective is likely to come across as pedantic or foolish.

Judgmental Perspective

A person habitually looking at life through this perspective will help you to feel horrible. She feels horrible herself and is happy to drag you down just when you need support. This type of person has a very non-constructive critical perspective. His or her criticism is not offered to help you do a better job. It is offered to make them feel one up and you one down.

Complicated Perspective

A person using this perspective will distract you from focusing on the issue at hand by scattering the conversation into all kinds of other places, some of which may be relevant while others are miles away. This tendency may or may not be intentional.

"Life-is-a-Problem" Perspective

A person employing this kind of perspective has personally developed a style of making anything that happens into a problem requiring a fix-it man or woman. Even when something pleasurable is occurring she will find a hidden conflict or agenda. A person with this perspective takes on the role of melodramatic victim in most situations and will invite you to be the same or make you the cause of her victimhood.

Black-and-White Perspective

One who takes on this perspective sees everything as right or wrong. There is no room for growth, compromise, or new understandings. If you are in disagreement with a person who perceives life through this perspective, expect to be cast into the role of villain.

Exclusive Perspective
One who views life with this perspective finds someone else to be the enemy. The enemy is classified as bad, and the person taking on this perspective is good. There is no room for compassion, meeting in the middle, or a loving resolution with this type of perspective. If someone tells you about his or her past relationship with this type of perspective, you could be setting yourself up to be the next enemy.

Problem-Oriented Perspective
Someone using this perspective will focus on problems instead of solutions. He will find the fault and hopelessness in each situation. Similar to someone with a negative perspective, he will create a way to help you feel stuck. The difference in his method is that he will not only focus on what is wrong with the present but cleverly plan steps to ensure that it will also be wrong in the future. You may wonder why he does this and what his purpose is, as it will make no sense to most.

Critical Perspective
While a person with a judgmental perspective will help you to *feel* awful, a person using a critical perspective will help you think that you *are* horrible. A person utilizing this perspective will give you many logical reasons to think of yourself as less than worthy.

Interruptive Perspective
Don't expect to have a conversation or be listened to when you speak to someone with this perspective. He is much more concerned with what he has to say than with what you have to say. He will step over your words with his

own, splash over your ideas with his more important ones, and tie your conversation into a knot with his lack of respect.

Fighter's Perspective

A person who uses this perspective is pointed toward a fight. He or she will escalate matters until they explode, looking for conflict and helping it to erupt. The methods may be verbal or physical. This perspective is volatile and dangerous. It is mandatory that you remove yourself from someone who is making this perspective his or her way of communicating. If you are prone to using this perspective, it is important that you get help.

Expense Humor Perspective

The person choosing this perspective will find humor at the expense of others' well-being. He may make you or others laugh, but in such a way that someone else will cry. If you are not the butt of these jokes today, you most likely will be tomorrow.

Don't Settle for a Degenerative Perspective In Your Relationship

Someone who habitually employs one of the degenerative perspectives loses most of life's opportunities because he or she is busy developing reasons for why proposed solutions cannot work. A degenerative perspective is the opposite of a generative perspective, which means giving birth to new life, feeding the next generation of moments, being generous. A person who is trapped in a degenerative perspective is addicted to being stuck and motionless for fear of feeling.

Once someone makes it apparent that their perspective is unhelpful, it is your responsibility to remove yourself from the relationship. Such a problem can last for a lifetime for no good reason. If you choose to commit yourself to a relationship with someone who has an unhelpful perspective, you have chosen to use a type of unhelpful perspective yourself. You are placing yourself in a predictable victim role.

Once you discover that someone offers an unhelpful perspective, you will benefit by releasing yourself from the relationship. Make sure that it's a regular occurrence before making a permanent decision. Check to see if your own perspective is making your partner look like the "bad guy," or if their perspective is truly abrasive to you on a regular basis.

If a person introduces a negative perspective to you at the outset of a relationship, you can pretty well assume that you will be hearing that perspective repeatedly. On the other hand, if someone who is ordinarily positive has an outburst of negative perspective from time to time during highly stressful situations, be forgiving and don't worry.

If you are entering a new relationship and are introduced to a person's destructive perspective, there is not a lot of reason to sign up for the effects it will soon have on you. If you hear yourself complaining internally or externally, take it as a valid warning sign. If you hear yourself complaining more than once about the same problem, it is your responsibility to invite your partner to change; if he or she doesn't decide to make an ongoing attempt with positive results, make a better partner choice. There is never a good reason to set yourself up for discomfort. If you do, it is you alone who is responsible for making that choice, not your partner.

If you have placed a lot of value on a relationship that has been serving you well in a variety of other ways for a significant segment of your life, it will certainly be worthwhile to ask your partner to make a change if their perspective is dragging you down. In a loving and constructive way, indicate to your partner that his or her perspective is often unhelpful to you, and ask if he or she would be willing to try another kind of perspective. Be very specific and focus on what you do want. Give your partner an opportunity to grow and become an emotional ally to you before choosing to end a long-term bond. See what he or she is able to accomplish before making a decision to leave.

HOW TO CHANGE YOUR OWN PERSPECTIVE
The 22-Day Life Turn-Around Practice

If you have one of the degenerative perspectives, you can practice changing it with the help of the following exercises. When you develop a generating perspective you will be happier and more likely to attract a happier mate, which is the basis of a healthy relationship.

Turning a Negative Perspective into a Positive One

Days one through six:

Do this practice every day at the same time. Pick a time during which you can commit to spend ten minutes writing. Choose a situation that you are currently viewing as negative. Use the time to write down positive aspects about that situation. Look for the good that is also present, the opportunities, the lessons, and the gifts.

Day seven:

Give yourself a rest from your journal-writing.

Days eight through thirteen:

Do this practice every day at the same time, and commit to spend ten minutes writing. During your daily ten minutes, make a list of anything that is good in your life. Think of people, situations, and things that have contributed positively to your life.

Day fourteen:

Take a rest from the journal-writing today.

Days fifteen through twenty:

Make it a habit to thank a minimum of one person a day for some way that they have contributed to you.

Day twenty–one:

Take a rest.

Days twenty-two and beyond:

Discipline your mind to focus on the positive aspects of each situation you encounter in your life. Also, stay focused on reasons to be grateful to others. When this becomes overly challenging, return to the journal-writing process to help yourself.

Turning a Falsely Educational Perspective into a Truly Educational Perspective

Days one through six:

Mark in your calendar one hour each week during which you will learn about something new. You can learn from books, movies, other people, classes, television, radio, or observation.

Day seven:

Make a list of people who might benefit from what you have learned. Choose times during your next week to make calls, emails, or personal contact so that you can ask people if they would be interested in hearing about what you learned.

Days eight through thirteen:

Carry out your planned calls, emails or personal contacts.

Day fourteen:

Take ten minutes to write about the positive effects of your experience.

Days fifteen through twenty:

Set a schedule during which you will repeat the exercises from days one through fourteen in a six-day time frame.

Day twenty-one:

Take a rest today.

Days twenty-two and beyond:

Make it a regular part of your life to learn and share new things. You can set up the schedule in any way that works for you. Some will opt to learn new things on a weekly basis, while some will be inspired go through major educational processes that take months, years, or even a lifetime.

Turning A Judgmental Perspective Into A Constructive Perspective

Day one:

Write down how you feel about your overall well-being or lack of it. How does your body feel? What is your comfort level in life? How often do you experience pleasure?

Days two through six:

Do this practice every day at the same time, and commit to spend five minutes writing. Think of ways to improve your health, your comfort, and your pleasure in life. Write down a way in which you can make your primary focus your own health and well-being on that day. After writing down your intention, add either "I will carry out this intention today because I matter," or "I will not carry out this intention today because I do not matter." Choose to carry the intention out or to use the same amount of energy to resist carrying the intention out.

Day seven:

Take a rest from the journal-writing today.

Days eight through thirteen:

Continue the practice you were doing during days two through six. In addition, during your writing time make a list of the ways that you were benefited or hurt by either carrying out or not carrying out your intentions.

Day fourteen:

Take a rest from the journal-writing today.

Days fifteen through twenty:

Each day, focus on sharing well-being with others. Spend ten minutes each night listing ways in which you contributed to others' well-being and how you felt afterwards. Also list ways in which you contributed to others' lack of well-being and how you felt afterwards.

Day twenty-one:

Take a break from journal-writing today.

Days twenty-two and beyond:

Invite yourself to create the well-being that makes your life a happy experience.

Turning A Complicated Perspective Into A Simple Perspective

Days one through six:

Do this practice every day at the same time, and commit to spend fifteen minutes writing. Use this time to refocus your understanding of a problem by answering the following questions.

1) What is the most recent problem I encountered?

2) If I had to define the problem in one sentence, what would that be?

3) If I had to define the problem in one word, what would that be?

4) If I had to define the solution in one sentence, what would that be?

5) If I had to define the solution in one word, what would that be?

Day seven:

Take a rest from the exercise.

Days eight through thirteen:

Continue the process and add the following questions to the exercise.

6) Keeping my response to #5 in mind, what are three simple things I can do to contribute to a favorable outcome to   this   problem?

7) Am I committed to doing these things?

8) By when?

Day fourteen:

Take a rest from the journal-writing today.

Days fifteen through twenty-one:

Repeat the process from days eight through thirteen.

Days twenty-two and beyond:

Discipline your mind to turn any problem you encounter into its simplest form before attempting to address it. Then turn your attention to positive responses to the problem. When this feels overly challenging, return to the journal-writing exercises.

Turning "Life-Is-A-Problem" to a "Life-Is-Good" Perspective

Days one through six:

Do this practice every day at the same time, and commit to spend fifteen minutes writing about a recent time during which you perceived yourself to be a victim. Think of another way that you could have responded to the situation so that you would not have been a victim. Write this down also.

Day seven:

Take a rest from the journal-writing today.

Days eight through thirteen:

Repeat the exercise you practiced during days one through six but instead write about significant times in your past during which you felt victimized.

Day fourteen:

Take a rest from journal-writing today.

Days fifteen through twenty:

Repeat the exercise you have been practicing with the following change: Given your current life circumstances and your mindset, predict times in the near future during which you might tend to see yourself as a victim. Design your new approach before the actual situation takes place.

Day twenty-one:

Take a rest from your journal-writing.

Days twenty-two and beyond:

Train your mind to look for a solution whenever you perceive yourself to be at the center of a problem. Any time that you find yourself feeling like a victim of a problem, make your mind focus on a solution. This is an in-the-moment exercise. When this seems overly challenging, resume the journal-writing process.

Turning Black and White to an All-And-Any-Shades Perspective

Days one through six:

Every time that you find yourself involved in a conflict with someone, whether in an intimate relationship or otherwise, say that you need some time to think before making a decision. Spend ten minutes alone writing down five positive or valid reasons why the other person has taken his or her position. Then write down five possible compromises. When you again engage the other person, consider your task to be that of finding a compromise instead of winning.

At the end of each day, write down what you felt and learned as a result of doing this practice.

Day seven:
Take a break from journal-writing today.

Days eight through thirteen:
Repeat the process you did in days one through six.

Day fourteen:
Take a break from journal-writing today.

Days fifteen through twenty:
Continue to repeat this process of dealing thoughtfully with conflict and being willing to compromise.

Day twenty-one:
Take a break from journal-writing today.

Days twenty-two and beyond:
Discipline your mind to look for the value of the other person's perspective as well as a compromise whenever you are faced with disagreement or conflict. When this seems overly challenging, resume the journal-writing process.

Turning an Exclusive to an Inclusive Perspective
Days one through six:
Do this practice every day at the same time and commit to spend ten minutes focusing on and writing about someone toward whom you feel superior. Answer the following questions about that person.

1) If I am jealous of this person, what is my jealousy about?

2) If I am scared of this person, what is my fear about?

3) If I am angry at this person, what is my anger about?

4) If I allow myself to admire this person, what are three things about him or her that I admire?

5) If I allow my goal to be finding a bridge of pleasurable communication with this person, how will I do it?

Day seven:

Take a break from journal-writing today.

Days eight through thirteen:

Do the same practice as the first week but now focus on and write about someone toward whom you feel inferior. Answer the following questions about yourself in relationship to that person.

1) If I allow myself to feel as wonderful as this person, what can I appreciate that is wonderful about me?

2) What might that person be admiring in me?

3) If I allow my goal to be finding a mutually empowering type of communication with this person, how will I do it?

Day fourteen:

Take a rest from journal-writing today.

Days fifteen through twenty:

Do this practice every day at the same time. Commit to spend fifteen minutes sitting in a quiet place with your eyes closed. During this time imagine a person with whom you have felt difficulty, awkwardness, or negative energy when working or playing together. Regardless of who is the source of this energy, imagine that a feeling of mutual respect and admiration is in the atmosphere. Picture yourself working or playing together in a way that is pleasurable and empowering to both of you.

Day twenty-one:

Take a rest from the exercise today.

Days twenty-two and beyond:

Discipline your heart to encounter all people as your valuable equals. When this seems overly challenging, resume the journal-writing and positive visualization process.

Turning an Interruptive to an Inquisitive Perspective

Days one through six:

Do this practice every day at the same time and commit to spend ten minutes writing. Make a list of times that you interrupted others during the past twenty-four hours.

Day seven:

Take a break from journal-writing today.

Days eight through thirteen:

Repeat the exercise you did during days one through six with the following addition. After each interruption that you record, write down another way that you could have responded if your goal had been to further the conversation in a mutually respectful and interactive way.

Day fourteen:

Take a rest from journal-writing today.

Days fifteen through twenty:

Next time you wish to interrupt, listen more carefully to what your partner or whoever you are speaking with is telling you. Listen in the way that you would listen to the most important teacher in the world. When she pauses, ask a question that invites her to talk even more about the topic. Use your ten minutes of daily writing time to make note of how it felt to do this.

Day twenty-one:

Take a rest from journal-writing today.

Days twenty-two and beyond:

Discipline your mind to make interactive communication more important than interruption. Whenever this seems overly challenging, return to the writing exercises for help.

Relationships with and without Compatible Perspectives

If you find yourself consistently trying to convince your partner to be a different person, you are not compatible in the perspective aspect of relationships. You might as well take out a can of green paint and try to change the color of the sky. The beauty of humanity lives in the diversity of perspectives. This is what allows for change, growth, and balance. If you are in a relationship with somebody whose perspective constantly clashes with yours, you are choosing a life of arguing. Philosophical debate is stimulating and can be positive if it is a minor part of your conversations. If it dominates your interactions, your home will become a frustrating and intellectual center instead of a nourishing place of replenishment.

If your perspectives are compatible you will find delight with the ways that the two of you complement each other. Your partner's words will touch your heart and contribute to your experience of day-to-day life. Partners with compatible perspectives report that they are each other's teachers and that they feel very at home with each other.

PERSPECTIVE IS THE INTERIOR DECORATION OF A RELATIONSHIP

When people paint their home and fill it with comfortable furniture and inspiring art, they are cozy yet energized. When the refrigerator is full of nourishing food and the garden is watered, the home-dwellers thrive. So it is with relationship perspective. Fill your mind and your partner's mind with uplifting and supportive stories. Then you will live in a flowering Queendom of wisteria, robin redbreast's songs, and warmth.

Chapter 3
COMMUNICATION
Connection in relationship

Communication is two hands holding that keep otherwise separate beings connected to each other. Communication can be made of warm vanilla pudding, but it can also be made of stale and moldy bread. Communication can surprise you when it is wrapped in velvet cloth but lined with used linen, full of holes, that someone else left in your partner's coat. Communication will delight you when you are expecting it to come in a basic bowl of beans and are offered a seven-course gourmet excursion.

Connected conceptually and energetically to the throat chakra—the chakra of communication—this area of relationship is clearly important to long-term success. How you choose to communicate determines the essence of your relationships. Communication within a relationship is a co-created map unique to that relationship. If you are happy with the map you have co-created, you will feel intimate and close to your partner. Ideally, you will experience your partner as your best friend.

It is possible to experience enjoyable communication from a partner regarding some aspects of your life while being dissatisfied with communication concerning other aspects. You live in a historic time during which it is common to desire perfect compatibility yet encounter ongoing disappointments. Things seem to work out for people in the movies, in the relationship books, and in fantasies. Unrealistic as this may be, you are likely to expect this from your own life yet feel that you fall short at times.

In the twenty-first century, traditional communication styles no longer work reliably, and new communication styles are in an experimental stage. Thus you are often digging out the path and traveling upon it at the same time, which can be challenging and rocky, but also studded with sometimes-buried precious stones. Good communication requires experimentation and creativity as well as patience.

MANY COMMUNICATION CHALLENGES CAN BE REMEDIED

Don't throw a relationship out because communication is difficult. Everyone can improve in this area. When two willing partners decide to improve communication with each other, miraculous results are possible. Although each person brings his or her own perspective to a relationship, communication is something that is developed together.

If you have a partner who communicates in a way that builds love and closeness, and this person is willing to address his or her own shortcomings, you have a good partner.   Tammy felt loved by her partner's generous actions, his affectionate way, and his sharing of personal experiences. When it came to asking her questions, however, Will was unskilled. Tammy complained that Will wouldn't know anything about her if she didn't talk so readily about herself. He never asked questions such as "How was your day? What did you feel about that? What's your opinion?" although he was an excellent listener whenever she volunteered information about herself.

Tammy's partner was willing to learn. He asked her for suggestions. "While questions are first nature to you, Tammy," Will said, "they are not to me. Nobody asked me questions when I was growing up. In fact, I learned that prying into another's business was rude.   But you're right, Tammy. Questions make us closer. I like all of the questions that you ask me."

Will practiced his new approach and the couple's communication improved significantly. It was necessary that Tammy practice patience in this situation and that she allow herself to be the teacher in this aspect of their relationship. You need not walk out the door when there are communication difficulties, because they are common and solvable if you have two participatory players. This mutual willingness is key.

Selina frequently praised her partner. When she got home from a long workday she still had plenty of attention to give to him as well as to return phone calls to friends. She generously hosted guests in their house but consistently made sure that he was her priority.

Bill loved this. "I've never had a girlfriend who could be a perfect balance of extrovert and introvert before," he said. "Plus she constantly compliments me. I feel great about myself. On the other hand, I feel unequal to her. She won't tell me how she's feeling so I have to use my imagination, which is often inaccurate. I'm not always sure about how to make her happy. She doesn't give me a lot of clues, so I have to guess and don't do a great job. I feel like I'm not giving enough to her, and I don't know how to."

Selina's side of the story differed from Bill's. She believed that Bill was happy to receive her care but was stingy about giving his own. "He doesn't make attempts to please me and make me feel good, even though he laps up my attention like an eager puppy dog."

On the other hand, his presence was very nurturing and his body fed her body. On a physical level he communicated safe and passionate warmth, but on a verbal and action level he communicated that he didn't know her well and didn't want to serve her. There was a lot of sweetness and love between this couple, but there was also great discontent on Selina's part and they were stuck.

This couple had the opportunity to develop wonderful and delightful communication in ways that were lacking by starting with the strength of successful communication in other areas. Selina had the opportunity to practice clarifying and asking for what she wanted. Unfortunately, she took the position that Bill didn't care and it was up to him. She wasn't willing to take a more active role in getting her needs met.

Her last boyfriend had been more attuned to her in that way, and she felt that Bill should be.

Bill, on the other hand, had his own limitations and discomforts. He wasn't willing to take a more active role in figuring out what made her happy by watching, listening, and sensing. He expected detailed directions and saw his only other option to be guessing. His opinion was that a change relied upon her. This couple broke up, both blaming each other for communication difficulties instead of utilizing the breakdown as an opportunity to develop deeper intimacy.

SOME COMMUNICATION DIFFICULTIES ARE INHERENT

While effort is important, personality style is also. Some people will naturally understand each other better. This is influenced by cultural upbringing, perspective type (see Chapter Two), creative personality type (read *Creative Intimacy*—see "Resources" section), and physical type (read about Ayurvedic types). If, for example, you were raised in a loud, expressive family and your partner grew up in a reserved family, it will influence the assumptions you each make about communication. In other words, you grew up with different expectations about how to communicate. If you perceive the world mostly through emotion and your partner perceives the world mostly through the intellect, you will encounter unexpected misunderstandings regarding your basic perceptions. If you are a light, highly energetic, spontaneous person you might feel very nurtured and safe with a grounded, steady, heavier, more structured person and very anxious with someone who shares your physical chemistry. Trust your overall sense of how the relationship feels experientially from the very beginning, because you can count on that feeling being with you for years to come when you choose someone as a mate.

COMMUNICATION COMPATIBILITY TEST

If you are deciding whether to enter a committed relationship with someone, you will want to make sure that your communication is a source of ongoing intimacy and closeness. There is no reason to be with someone if you are co-creating distance and upset unless you are working at remedying this. The following test will assist you in determining how compatible you are with your potential mate in the area of communication. Read each statement and choose the one that most closely represents you. Score your relationship on a continuum of **-4 to 4.**

-4 We are very scared of each other, or one of us is scared of the other. The damage done is not reparable.

-3 Both or one of us feel deeply hurt by the other's communication. We are resentful and angry toward each other.

-2 Basically we both feel alone, although we are in a relationship together.

-1 We meet most of our needs outside the relationship so we are two generally happy people who live together. Since our honeymoon phase was good, we still like each other and have some good interactions here and there.

0 We live together. It works. Neither of us really wanted anything spectacular out of life. No problems. Nothing great.

1 We meet certain needs for each other but are also very disappointed in a variety of ways.

2 We meet a lot of needs for each other and have settled in a lot of ways. Settling is okay. We are both content. There is understanding between us.

3 We meet many needs for each other and are happy with each other. We have learned to serve each other well.

4 We meet many communication needs for each other and are profoundly grateful to have each other as our most intimate, close friend. We have taken the time to get to know each other very well and give to each other so that we both prosper and feel happy.

Understanding Your Score

-4 to -2 Your relationship does not serve you. It is time to get help and make a big change or separate.

-1 to 0 You can do better. Do you really want to live like this? It's up to you. Getting help or breaking up are options if you want to be more fulfilled.

1-2 Your relationship is adequate, but you can make it wonderful by learning to improve your communication with each other.

3-4 Congratulations. You have given yourself a wonderful gift. You and your partner have co-created very special communication.

COMMUNICATION EXISTS IN MANY FORMS

If you are not as fulfilled with your communication as you would like to be, it will help you to clarify which aspect of your communication is not pleasing to you. Communication is the basis of being close, and it is happening all the time, whether or not we are in a verbal conversation. You communicate in all the ways listed below:

words
actions
thoughts
gifts
food
work away from home
your work at home
treatment of important people outside the relationship
plans
money
energy
attention
humor
warmth

romance
consistency
spontaneity
time
your appearance
body language
affection
sexuality
prayers
silence
questions
answers
emotions
dream states
breathing
insights

By reviewing different types of communication you will get ideas about how to improve your communication and ways to ask your partner to improve his or hers. You might also be able to clarify why a relationship isn't serving you, and what you want to do about that. It will be helpful to make lists of desires and requests you have of your mate and exchange the lists. Responding to a partner's needs is a service that makes a relationship wonderful.

Heather knew that she was dissatisfied with Harriet's communication, but she wasn't sure why. By utilizing the above list she realized that Harriet's body language was distancing to her. Although Harriet was very affectionate with her words, her body language often gave a different message.

Harriet knew exactly what Heather was referring to once Heather brought it up. Harriet grew up in a family where body language was stiff, and physical affection was rarely expressed. Harriet was glad that Heather brought up this topic because she herself was uncomfortable with her body language habits and wanted to practice being more affectionate. Once the communication complaint was clear and out on the table, something could be done that served both partners. Heather agreed to help Harriet with being more affectionate by initiating more affection herself. Both Heather and Harriet prospered.

VERBAL COMMUNICATION SERVES MANY PURPOSES

Verbal communication is used for a variety of purposes in a relationship. It is important to master each of the following skills in a way that is clear to your loved one.

support
encouragement
understanding
sympathy
seduction
praise
comfort
help
alteration
information
plans
pleasure
warmth
requests
mood

If you are disappointed with the communication in your relationship but unsure why, you can use this list of communication purposes to identify what is lacking. Donna was upset with the communication between Roy and her but could not clarify why. By reviewing the list of communication purposes she became aware that Roy often made requests that were unclear and subtle to her. For example, when he was hoping that they could spend the holidays privately without family, he talked about how much he loved sunshine. She didn't realize that he was hinting about going out of town together until it was too late to make a practical plan. She assumed that he was just commenting on how much he missed the summer.

Once Donna was clear about her frustration, she could ask Roy to be direct in his communication. His communication pattern was so habitual that it hadn't occurred to him to be direct. He grew up in a family in which nobody was direct. Offered the possibility of positive change, Roy felt inspired. He decided to become a direct communicator, and over time he improved his relationship with Donna as well as everyone else in his life.

SUPPORTIVE VS. NON-SUPPORTIVE COMMUNICATION

Ophelia often told her mate, John, that she found his motives to be very pure. She let him know that in her eyes he was a very good person.

John, on the other hand, often doubted Ophelia, advising her to change the way that she went about life (even though her ways worked well for her) and questioning her motives as though she were unconsciously misdirected. While Ophelia was genuinely able to support John's basic nature, John was not doing this for her. Through counseling John came to realize that he was feeling competitive toward his wife. He didn't feel as good about himself as she did, and he relieved himself of his anxiety by doubting and directing her.

Because John was humble and dedicated to his relationship, he was able to see this and make a conscious shift. If one person is feeling unsupported and the other is willing to make his or her role in the relationship more positive, there are ways to alter the problem.

Exercise for Developing Support in a Relationship
This exercise is designed for two.

1) Both of you write down one way in which you would like to be supported by the other. Be specific.

2) Both of you practice supporting the other in exactly the way requested.

3) Repeat this exercise every day for one month.

4) Once a week talk about your experience of the exercise.

5) After one month continue the process once a week regularly.

VERBAL ENCOURAGEMENT VS. LACK OF VERBAL ENCOURAGEMENT

Verbal encouragement is another healthy and necessary vitamin in a relationship. George consistently encouraged his wife to succeed at whatever she set out to do. "You will definitely get that job done. You'll pass your nursing exam on the first try. I'm sure you can. How can I help you to study?"

Jeannie felt very encouraged by her husband. George, on the other hand, did not feel encouraged by Jeannie. When he tried to set schedules for meeting his goals, she ignored this and made other social plans, expecting him to participate. When he struggled to get something done she agreed with his own fears, making statements such as "Maybe it's too hard for you, George."

George and Jeannie came to counseling. Since we all have particular communication skills that are strong and others that are weak, a relationship is a great ground for improvement. You can teach each other in areas of strength while benefiting from each other in areas of weakness, as long as the weaknesses don't match. When they do, situations can be very straining, but with education and help they can be turned around as well.

Unfortunately, Jeannie was too embarrassed to admit that something she was doing was unhelpful. Coming from a family in which the father constantly criticized the mother and the mother went along with it, behaving like a second-class citizen, Jeannie was unwilling to accept any criticism.

Consequently, this couple missed the opportunity to make wonderful changes. George felt let down by Jeannie's inability to change, and Jeannie felt let down by his disappointment in her.

Mutual encouragement is a must in a good relationship. Your partner affects your concept of yourself, your motivation level, and your success, and vice versa. If encouragement is a weakness in your relationship, the following exercise can benefit you.

Exercise for Developing Encouragement in a Relationship

This exercise is designed for two.

1) Both of you make a list of all the things that are important to your partner: all that he or she wants to accomplish, feel, do, and be.

2) Trade lists and add on anything that your partner missed about you.

3) Every day for two weeks, both of you choose one item from the list and make it a point to encourage your partner in that way.

4) Both of you number your lists from most important to least important.

5) Every day for two weeks, both of you make sure to encourage your partner on his or her three top priorities.

6) Discuss the benefits experienced over the past month.

UNDERSTANDING VS. MISUNDERSTANDING

Understanding is a critical element of verbal communication. When you understand, you position yourself "below someone's ground." In other words, you give them a foundation. Understanding need not be of an analytical nature. Sometimes you just wish to know that you are being seen, heard, or felt by a non-evaluating witness. Babies thrive on being seen, heard, and felt without analysis. As an adult you continue to require this type of attention but rarely get enough of it. Butch loved his relationship because TJ liked to listen to him and reflect back to him what he said in a way that made him feel known. TJ loved the relationship because he experienced the same treatment from Butch.

If you are lacking understanding in a relationship, take turns talking and listening. TJ and Butch explained that they give each other time to talk without imposing self-centered ideas or advice on each other's individual life process. Their style involves simply absorbing what the other is saying from his perspective and reflecting it back to him. For example, Butch told TJ that he had a very happy day going to the beach with his two closest friends outside the relationship, and that time away from home gave him a lot of energy to bring back to the relationship.

"So you felt really happy when you went to the beach with Lindsay and Glen. I'm happy when you are happy," was TJ's response.

Cynthia and Darron had a habit of advising and competing in place of understanding. Cynthia often wanted personal attention after work. She told Darron that she liked to share news about her day, be touched, and be admired. Darron, however, made it a daily habit to give Cynthia advice about the many ways in which she could improve her personality and life. Cynthia became thin and anxious during the course of that relationship. She felt like she was being picked at and eaten up.

Darron liked to share his accomplishments and pleasurable experiences. He would have preferred it if Cynthia responded by listening and expressing joy and respect for him. Instead, his sharing of himself most often elicited a response about what was even better in her life. By the end of their relationship he had gained thirty pounds. He felt like he was carrying an insecure part of Cynthia in his own body.

If your relationship is suffering from lack of understanding, you have the opportunity to remedy this.

Exercise for Developing Understanding in a Relationship

You can agree to do this entire exercise together, or one of you can start the process. Either way will initiate changes.

1) Figure out if you are feeling a desire to be heard more often, seen more often, physically touched more often, or emotionally felt more often.

2) Clarify on paper how you want your partner to demonstrate that he or she hears, sees, physically receives, or emotionally feels you.

3) Ask your partner to read what you have written. Invite him or her to respond to your request every day for a week.

4) Each evening spend a few minutes thanking your partner for ways in which he or she has responded to what you requested. If necessary, provide more detailed information in order to help your partner meet your requests.

PRAISE VS. ISOLATION

Praise is another important ingredient in a relationship. There are many things to praise everyone about (just like there is always something to criticize if you are seeking that). If you focus on what you like in others, you will have continuous praise to give. As a person who constantly notices the good in others but is a little shy, I have learned that it is important to speak my lists of gratitude out loud. When I do this people feel happy about themselves and more inclined to see the good in others.

Martine and Frank were miserable with each other, and life together kept getting worse. They decided to give each other a compliment at the beginning and end of each day, and it worked wonders. This little formula turned things around quickly. If there is not enough praise in your relationship, begin to compliment your mate for things you like about him or her. Notice the things that your partner says, does, wears, feels, etc., that you appreciate. The more you put your mind to this, the more you will find yourself living in a natural state of appreciation. When you feel appreciative, you are more inclined to be generous with your attention and time.

Ed and Caitlin rarely complimented each other after the first few months of their relationship passed. Although they shared many activities and interesting discussions, their passion dwindled so they went to counseling. Both had the attitude that compliments were corny, and they resisted incorporating praise into their regular conversations. As a result, their passion for each other went flat and they broke up.

If praise is lacking in your relationship, practice is needed. The following exercise will bring praise into your relationship.

Exercise for Developing Praise in a Relationship
This exercise can be done by both partners or by one.

1) Every night before going to sleep, write down three things that you appreciate, admire, or enjoy about your partner.

2) Tell your partner what you wrote down.

3) Repeat this process for a month.

4) After a month, repeat this process once a week on a regular basis.

HELP VS. NEGLECT
A relationship requires that you and your mate offer each other help. A relationship in which help is not offered is like a pumping heart and set of veins with no blood moving back and forth between them. Be conscious of the many responsibilities that your mate takes on, and lessen his or her load by offering help.

Sally took care of her boyfriend Kevin's taxes every year because she liked to give to him. When Sally moved from her studio to an apartment, Kevin rented movers to help her because he cared deeply about her. Sally took Kevin shopping for a new bedroom throw rug and some warm slippers. Whenever Sally worked late at night she came home to a warm meal cooked by Kevin. Sally and Kevin assumed roles of actively giving to each other from day one of their relationship. When they first met, Sally was in the middle of studying for finals, and Kevin cooked dinner for her every night. At that time Kevin was going through a very challenging period because his mother had just died, so Sally spent lots of time just holding him while he cried and told stories about his mother. Even though she had finals coming up, she gave Kevin a listening ear and heart whenever he needed it. Even though Kevin was at the depth of despair, he came home from a long workday and prepared a three-course meal for Sally and did her laundry. This couple communicated their love for one another through actions that built a very sturdy, loving relationship.

Geraldine was constantly worried that she wouldn't have time to meet all of her career goals, take care of her body, eat well, and give herself ample time for a good social life. Consequently, she did not do anything extra for her boyfriend, Charlie. They talked on the phone, cooked meals together, went out together, and took care of their own needs solely. Charlie felt that his career was more important than his relationship. At work he was generous with his actions, always going the extra nine yards to make a co-worker or client feel at home in his network marketing business. He was willing to stay late to help someone out even if their needs were not work-related. Charlie drove people if their car broke down, counseled people who had personal problems, and often picked up lunch for everyone in the office. Charlie overextended himself to friends in the same way, becoming known as a giver both at work and in his social circles. By the time he got home he had little to give to himself and consequently very little to give to Geraldine. He did shower her with affection and physical passion. He told her how much he loved her and listened caringly to what she had to say. Their relationship fell apart, however, because neither of them offered love through action. Both felt uncared for and neglected in the end.

Exercise for Developing Help in a Relationship
This exercise is designed for two.
1) Both of you write down something that your partner can actively do to help you out in the next 24 hours.
2) Tell each other what you wrote down.
3) Do it.
4) Repeat this exercise every day for two weeks.
5) After two weeks, repeat this exercise twice a week on an ongoing basis.

THE ART OF ALTERING VS. THE ACT OF ACCUSING

Nobody can live without making mistakes. That is why offering a new perspective or a new approach to a partner can be a precious gift. It is from another's communication that we expand our viewpoint and improve our ways of doing things.

Norman noticed that his partner Gloria made messes frequently when trying to fix things in the house. Gloria left holes in the wall after a poor attempt to put up some artwork. She left paint on the sink after repainting the bathroom. She tore the flannel sheets when they were only two months old. Norman watched his partner compassionately and realized that Gloria did these kinds of things when she was feeling nervous.

Norman decided to join his partner next time she made a house repair. He went to the store with Gloria to pick out tiles to replace ones that had chipped. Norman told Gloria that whenever he worked on household tasks he practiced breathing deeply and making the work into a meditation. He invited Gloria to join him. Gloria accepted the invitation, which was very lovingly presented. With Norman's care and guidance she calmed down and did better with household tasks.

Gabriel was annoyed by the way that Sara cleaned house and constantly told her so. "You're a terrible sweeper. These dishes look like they should still be in the dishwasher. This bed feels like it was made by a child." Gabriel's communication was an attempt to alter unfavorable situations but it infuriated Sara and, not surprisingly, her actions remained the same. The warmth between them diminished.

As partners we have the opportunity to redirect each other. When we do this with love, we strengthen our bond. When we do this with anger or judgment, we deplete our bond. If the art of altering in a loving way is missing from your relationship, the following exercise will be beneficial.

Exercise for Developing the Art of Altering

You can do this exercise together, or one of you can do it.

1) Write down something that you would like your partner to be able to do more adequately, easily, or comfortably.

2) Think of three ways that you can kindly and supportively assist him or her in doing so.

3) Try out one of your ideas. If your partner is receptive, great. If not, find out why. Be humble enough to get feedback. It is possible that you are coming across as critical, or that your partner is not interested in improving in this area.

4) If the feedback indicates that you were being critical, try again in another way at another time. If the feedback indicates that your partner is not interested in improving in this area, let it go and redirect your energy.

AWARENESS VS. LACK OF INFORMATION

Sharing information is an important part of communication. Kendra never ended a day without making sure that her partner knew everything that was important for him to know. She told him how she was feeling and how much she appreciated him. She told him about anything practical that she had thought about during the day that he would need to know, including invitations to events, and questions or ideas relating to financial issues. Seth did the same with Kendra. As a result, both members of the couple reported that they felt part of a team.

Dolly often let days go by before sharing that she was unhappy with something Stewart did. Stewart frequently neglected to inform Dolly of important matters regarding their finances, phone messages, and his individual plans. Both participants in this marriage felt isolated and alone.

It is important to treat partnership like a team with common purposes, especially when living together. Don't assume that your partner knows anything regarding you and your life together unless you communicate directly. If sharing of information is lacking in your relationship, the following exercise will help to improve your situation.

Exercise for Better Imparting Information

This exercise is designed to do together.

1) Each night spend twenty minutes reporting to each other on the following topics: scheduling, plans, feelings, decisions, important thoughts.

2) Repeat this exercise every night for two weeks.

3) Discuss the benefits you have gained at the end of the two weeks.

4) Decide on a schedule including an amount of time, a set time, and set days to continue this process on a regular basis.

PLANNING TOGETHER VS. SELFISHNESS

Relationships require that plans be made together. Jason decided that he wanted to go to Sweden. Jason and Claire had very different financial situations. Jason booked a flight and trip without talking to Claire about it. He then invited Claire to go but expected her to come up with $4000. Claire was in the initial stages of getting a business going. Claire was very generous with money and often spent a lot on Jason in proportion to her income. Jason made five times as much money as Claire and had thirty times as much in savings. Nevertheless, Jason made his plans with only his needs and desires in mind.

When Claire declined to go on the trip and explained why, Jason made plans to go with another woman who had a higher income and could pay for her own trip. "She's just a good friend," he said. Claire, needless to say, lost interest in the relationship and ended it. Jason felt let down by Claire.

Belinda and William were in a similar situation. Belinda really wanted to go to Italy and booked a trip in hopes that William would be delighted to accompany her. After surprising William with the news, Belinda learned that William felt uncomfortable about spending that much money. Belinda offered to pay for half of William's trip or to change the trip to something that was more affordable for him. William was very grateful to accept her offer and ended up paying for all of their meals on a wonderful vacation.

A partnership is based on putting the strengths and weaknesses of two people together, sharing what each of you has, and making decisions that honor both of your desires and needs. You can't prepare for singlehood and be in a relationship at the same time. Either you are in or out. If your relationship suffers from lack of shared planning, the following exercise will be of great use.

Exercise for Remembering to Plan Together
This exercise is designed for two.

1) From now on, any time there is any type of decision to make, write it down and postpone the decision until you talk it over with your partner.

2) When discussing it, assume that both of your needs and desires are equally important. Make decisions based on compromise and honoring of each other's wishes and requirements.

REQUESTING VS. RESENTING

A relationship provides ample opportunities to make a request. Whenever Lewis wanted something he asked for it. "I would really like it if you would be willing to drive tonight. I'm tired. Are you willing to drive or are you tired also?" Or, "I would love to cuddle with you. Will you cuddle with me?"

Whenever Tracy wanted something she also asked. "I had a long day. Would you cook dinner for us tonight?" "I need some affection. Will you be close to me?"

This couple had an aura of well-being around them. Both members said that their needs were frequently met.

Sharon, on the other hand, felt uncomfortable about asking for anything and resented the fact that Ted often did. Ted felt Sharon's disapproval whenever he asked for what he wanted. This couple stayed miserably married for decades.

In order for your relationship to be effective it is necessary that both of you ask for what you want. Wanting without asking often leads to unfair resentment because your partner is not a mind reader. It is also important to acknowledge that your partner might not want to or be able to give you what you want, to the degree that you want it. This is where the art of acceptable compromise comes in. But first you must communicate your needs and desires, putting them squarely on the table without blame or threat.

The following exercise will help you to ask for what you want if your relationship has been weakened by not already doing this.

Exercise for Incorporating Requests

This exercise can be done by two or one.

1) Once a day take ten minutes to write down a request that you have of your partner. The form below might help you with this process.

2) Make that request within eight hours of writing it down.

3) Repeat this exercise every day for two weeks.
4) Write down any positive effects you experience from doing this each day.

Form for Clarifying a Responsible Request
Right now I feel_____. The only person responsible for my feelings is me. To let my feelings out today   in   a   healthy   way   I will_____. Something I want today is_____. Can I give it to myself? Does it require the generosity of another? Is the other I am thinking of my mate? What is the simplest way to ask my mate or someone else for what I want?

_____

_____. If they say yes, how will   I   express   my   appreciation? _____. If they say no, who can I ask for help instead?_____.

Relationships with and without Compatible Communication
If you experience repeated frustration when trying to talk to your mate, you are not compatible in the realm of communication. If you often feel misunderstood, unacknowledged, unseen, and unheard, you are not compatible. If you are overworking to get yourself across, you are not compatible. If your mate experiences any of the above difficulties, you are not compatible.

Communication is an adventure of learning, and in the best of relationships, misunderstandings can lead to deeper knowing of each other and self. Such a relationship composed of two partners who are compatible will exhibit pleasurable qualities. Both partners will feel that their mate knows them and understands them.

Both partners will feel unalone in the world.

COMMUNICATION IS EVER-PRESENT

Communication can glide lightly like little laughs, white butterfly wings, and maple seed pods twirling toward the ground. Communication can fall heavily like big boots filled with slush and cold mud. Communication is ever-present. Communication wakes you up with the sunrise, joins you in a morning embrace, looks back at you from the mirror while you brush your teeth, and escorts you out the door. She will never leave. You can bathe her with orchid amber soap and dress her in soft felt, or you can let her run wild and naked. There are many ways to make her happy, and as long as you make communication happy she will adore you.

With two of you it is a bit more tricky. Not only are you speaking to yourself and spirit with each breath, you are connecting to an entirely other universe. Do your best and you will find heavenly scents, wondrous surprises, warm bubble baths, and a life with a mate that is well worth waking up to each morning.

Chapter 4

Love
the heart in relationship

Love's eyes are sweet with the perspective of centuries. Love leaves the poetry of your heart naked when she wraps her brunette hair around your bare-skinned back. Who delights when she has her arms around love's chest? Who laughs with pleasure when he finds his love nested in her thoughts?

Love is the caterpillar fully protected and safe in the cocoon, yet her expression is the butterfly's wings. Love slips inside of you, secure and sturdy. Love splashes and sings with full abandon.

Who knows the truth about love? Is love blind or the eye of the soul? Does love come when you least expect it, or when you build a home and welcome her with outstretched arms? Does love conquer all or does love bring even the worst of enemies together? Do you pay a price for love or is love free? Is love in every maple tree, on every street corner, within each breath, or is love a buried treasure for those who dig diligently? Does love ever die, or does it just get reborn in a new form? If you fall in love with life are you Spirit's servant or a crazed narcissist? Can you love another without loving yourself? Can you love Spirit without loving another?

Like the heart chakra itself, love is at the center of everything. The absence of love is fear. At the center of every transaction, interaction, action, and lack of action is either love or fear. When love is present, grace, perspective, communication, well-being, passion, and practical life feel good. When fear is present, these elements feel uncomfortable.

With love, grace is felt in awe and gratitude. With love, one's partner is seen as a precious gift from Spirit, whereas with fear one's partner is seen as an obstacle. With love, one sees the opportunity involved in all of life's experiences. With fear, life's experiences lead to disappointment and cynicism. With love, communication fills us with delight and brings us close. With fear, communication creates distance and suffering. With love, power is a source of strength for everyone involved and keeps us alive. With fear, power turns in on itself and causes us disease. With love, passion is an exquisite and delicious dance. With fear, passion becomes hatred and anger. With love, we nourish ourselves and each other. With fear, we deprive ourselves of our basic needs. With love, practical life is based on service, striving toward perfection, and workability. With fear, practical life becomes messy and faulty.

The only thing in the way of love is lack of trust and willingness due to miseducation. By releasing the disappointments and fears created from unfortunate experiences and learning that love is the only safety, everyone can become a loving person. A loving person is not hungry for love nor does she search for love, because love is present wherever she turns.

When Joy met Marvin her heart felt fuller than ever before. She had no words to explain this. Her love for him overtook her. When Marvin met Joy he felt that her voice brought forth a hidden hunger in his heart and filled it at the same time. He could never explain why. Years later after up and downs, good times and bad times, problems met with solutions, and problems left dangling, this initial love remained.

Like Joy and Marvin, love can come in a second, but love also can be discovered over time. Three generations back, Marvin's great-grandparents were put together in an arranged marriage. Unlike Marvin, they did not experience love in the glance of initial contact. Time, however, brought great love to them. Through daily living they fell in love and experienced love throughout their life together.

The people who taught me the most about love years before I fell into love with a partner were my own parents, Cory and Ralph. After Mom died I received a letter that she had written to my sister, brother, and me shortly before she left her body. The letter said that the most fulfilling part of her journey on Earth had been loving her three children. My mother taught me how to return to a state of love in any situation by giving love to me. Shortly before my mother died it became apparent to me that the love I felt in my heart all of the time even when life was very scary or painful was the result of my parents' love. My mother sent her love to me wherever I was. My father loved me wherever I went. It would be a lie to say we didn't have struggles. We had struggles throughout my life, but love was never in question. Love was completely dependable, and for this I am eternally thankful.

My mother bounced back to a state of love regardless of any problem. I learned from her that finding one's own love is the basis of finding a positive answer to any difficulty. While grace, perspective, communication, well-being, passion, and practicality are all vital components of a good companionship, without love they are nothing and with love they are everything.

If you are in a relationship without love then you have either not learned to receive love or not learned to give love, or decided that you are a saint who needs to be loving under adverse conditions. If you fall into any of these categories you are depriving yourself of the most basic and important ingredient of a joyful and solid relationship.

In the other chapters of this book, a test is offered to help you see where you are in terms of fulfilling necessary requirements for having a good relationship. Unlike the other tests in this book, the love test only has two options, not a continuum of experience.

RELATIONSHIP LOVE TEST
Choose the statement that most applies to you. Your score is either 1 or 0.

0 I do not feel loved and/or loving on a daily basis in my relationship.

1 I feel loved and loving on a daily basis in my relationship. We do well or adequately at turning passages of fear back into passages of love.

Understanding Your Score

1 If you scored a one on this test, you are experiencing the most precious gift of life. Your relationship contains what it needs in the area of the heart.

0 If you scored a 0 on this test you have the opportunity to make a change. Regardless of your background, disappointments, or bad luck, love is available to you. You can receive and give limitless experiences of love as soon as you choose to do so.

THE ROADS TO LOVE

There are many roads to travel upon in love. Love is not at the end of exertion, struggle, or trouble. Love is always here and now when you choose to breathe it in and out. Forget about outcomes, destinations, and endings. See life as an ongoing opportunity to create new beginnings. Create these beginnings in love, and love will honor you, dine with you, court you, massage you, and bathe you.

One road of love is the road of kindness. Make kindness a daily practice. Be kind every time you have the opportunity to interact with another. Be kind each time you think a thought to yourself. Be kind in your mind. Be kind with your actions. Be kind with your words. Be kind with yourself. Practice this all the time, and love will fill your heart.

Another way to live in love is to practice forgiveness. Forgive every time you have the opportunity to do so. As soon as you think a thought of revenge, arrogance, or anger, immediately substitute it with a thought of forgiveness. Practice this all the time, and love will bloom in your heart.

To dance with love is to practice generosity. Be generous with others. Be generous with yourself. Any time you think a thought of despair, disappointment, lack, or envy, immediately replace it with a thought or action of generosity and gratitude. Train your heart to speak only of giving, your hands only to give, and love will shower you.

To make love your home is to practice joy. Substitute all thoughts of resentment or frustration with a solution pointing you right back to joy. Only allow your mind to think upon those things that nurture you, delight you, and support you, and love will become your nature.

Tools for Returning to Love
Practice kindness
Practice forgiveness
Practice generosity
Practice joy

Relationships with and without Compatible Love
Partners who do not love each other are not happy, fulfilled, or inspired to grow. Partners in love find meaning in living, find impetus to work through challenges, and find warmth of heart in being together.

LOVE IS COMPLETE
Love is simple. Why does love last in the hearts of some who have gone through the most horrific circumstances? Because love is eternal while circumstances are ephemeral. Love is free. Love is for everyone. Once you live in love, anything else becomes less fulfilling. Take one step toward love and love takes one step toward you. Make all circumstances opportunities to love, and love will be all you know.

Chapter 5

Emotional Chemistry
well-being in relationship

Mix milk with chocolate and you have a delicious-tasting beverage. Mix the orange juice with chocolate and your dinner guests won't return. So it is with emotional chemistry. Tea rose, vanilla, amber, and sandalwood mixed together make a woman smell like a beautiful garden. Tea rose, anise, patchouli, and sarsparilla mixed together may send suitors out the door. Rudolf Steiner discovered that if you plant beets next to carrots they thrive, but if you plant them next to garlic they don't do as well. Certain members of the vegetable kingdom prosper when growing side by side while others lose vitality. People are the same way. You will find that you become energized around particular people and depleted around others. With one friend you feel peaceful; with another you feel excited. It is important to choose a mate with whom you can feel both enlivened and comfortable, inspired yet grounded, calm yet passionate.

Your emotional chemistry with someone is a given. It is very hard to change. If you are not happy with the general feeling you get when living with your partner, then you're not in the right relationship. However, it is important to identify your own role in feeling anxiety or depression before blaming someone else. If you have a tendency to feel stressed or shut down, address that first. Then you will get a more realistic picture of the emotional chemistry between you and a partner.

ADDRESSING ANXIETY AND STRESS

There are many ways to alleviate anxiety. Exercise and diet are fundamental. It's also vital to have an outlet for your emotions. Living a life that you desire by choosing a career, friends, activities, and home that bring you joy is another factor in maintaining a life of low stress and minimal depression. Depression is caused by resisting one's natural feelings and inclinations. Anxiety is caused by putting a part of oneself on overdrive at the expense of another part. By living a balanced life in which the needs of your physical body, mind, emotional body, and soul are addressed   you will relieve yourself of anxiety and depression and feel happier as an individual. Then you will be more likely to attract a happy mate and enjoy the chemistry that is created when the two of you are together.

WELL-BEING
Some people feel that they would die for love, but love is something to live for. What good is human love when you are dead? We have eternity to be with Spirit, but it is in flesh on Earth that we experience the pleasures of human love. Our well-being is experienced in a properly nourished body and healthy environment. The foods we eat, the air we breathe, the money we receive and let go, the care we give to our bodies, the home in which we live, and the nature that we surround ourselves with all contribute to our well-being. It is important that a partner contributes to your well-being too.

WELL-BEING COMPATIBILITY TEST
The following test will assist you in determining how compatible you are with your potential mate in the area of well-being. Score your test on a continuum of -19 to 19.

Check all that apply:
Since entering this relationship I am…
more fit
eating better
feeling more healthy
living on more money
budgeting better
living in a cleaner home
living in a more esthetically pleasing home
breathing more clean air
feeling more nourished
getting better rest

feeling more energized
feeling more alert
feeling more inspired
feeling more peaceful
feeling more enthusiastic
feeling more passionate
being more productive
being more constructive
being more disciplined

Add 1 to your score for each of the above that you checked.

Check all that apply:
Since entering this relationship I am…
less fit
eating worse
feeling less healthy
living on less money
budgeting worse
living in a less clean home
living in a less esthetically pleasing home
breathing less clean air
feeling less nourished
feeling less energized
feeling less alert
feeling less inspired
feeling less peaceful
feeling less enthusiastic
feeling less passionate
being less productive
being less constructive
being less disciplined

Subtract 1 from your score for each of the above that you checked.

If you find yourself experiencing about the same level of well-being in any of the above categories (i.e., you are feeling as healthy within the relationship as you were before it), then mark a zero for that category and realize all is well in this particular category.

Check all that apply:
Since entering this relationship I am...
as fit
eating the same
feeling equally healthy
living on the same amount of money
budgeting the same
living in a house that is equally as clean as my last home
living in an equally aesthetic home
breathing equally clean air
feeling equally nourished
getting equal rest
feeling equally energized
feeling equally alert
feeling equally inspired
feeling equally peaceful
feeling equally enthusiastic
feeling equally passionate
being equally productive
being equally constructive
being equally disciplined
Add 0 for each of the above checked to your score.

Understanding Your Score
-19 to -1 This is not an adequate relationship for you. This relationship lowers your well-being.
0 to 19 This relationship supports your well-being. If you scored 1 on at least one item but scored -1 on others, you will benefit by learning to improve in the negative areas.

PRACTICAL IMPROVEMENT OF WELL-BEING

Improvement in any of these areas will require focus, assistance, and/or education. For example, if you are less financially stable as a couple than you were separately, you will want to get information or consultation from someone who is knowledgeable about money. Well-being can be disturbed by practical mistakes as well as psychological ones.

The well-being of a relationship will improve any time that one person independently chooses to make a change for the better. For example, Karla and Brent both complained that their energy levels had gone down since moving in together. Both said that their exercise programs had gone down the drain. Karla made an independent decision to get back on track by going to dance class three times a week and doing yoga for thirty minutes every morning. Within a week she was feeling very energetic and lively. This rubbed off on Brent, who began to feel better himself and, as a result, got back to his own exercise routine.

If the chemistry between the two of you is peaceful and passionate, and both of you have life habits that maintain a state of well-being when you are each alone, your relationship has everything it needs to work. Your job is to keep it working by treating each other appropriately. If a well-being breakdown occurs, one or both of you will need to change your behavior.

CAUSES OF BREAKDOWN IN WELL-BEING

The following common causes of breakdown may help you determine the source of a problem. Once you are clear about this, you will be positioned to invent a practical solution.

One partner was ill. The other did not help.

One partner was overworked. The other did not help.

One partner gave surprises and gifts regularly. The other did not.

One partner cooked, cleaned, massaged, and listened often. The other did not.

One partner paid for everything. The other paid for nothing.

One partner planned activities for both. The other did not.

One partner helped the other with her/his projects. The other did not.

One partner supported the other at achieving her/his goals. The other did not.

One partner made compromises for the other's happiness. The other did not.

One partner kept his word. The other did not.

One partner contributed to the house by gardening, painting, building, or paying others to do so. The other did not.

One partner made decisions after talking to the other partner. The other made solo decisions.

One partner encouraged both work and rest. The other insisted on working or resting 90-100 percent of the time.

One partner included the other's friends and family in plans and hosting. The other did not.

One partner made holiday plans. The other did not.

One partner realized when the other was upset and helped. The other did not.

One partner planned vacations. The other did not.

One partner took most of the responsibility for the children.

One partner initiated conversations. The other did not.

One partner initiated humor. The other did not.

One partner initiated playfulness. The other did not.

One partner was positive about addressing conflict and resolution. The other was not.

One partner frequently acknowledged the other's virtues. The other did not.

One partner attended to the couple's health insurance, life insurance, and other important matters. The other did not.

One partner handled the bills and budget. The other did not.

One partner bought a home. The other did not contribute.

RESTORING WELL-BEING IN A RELATIONSHIP AFTER A BREAKDOWN

Once you have identified the source of the breakdown you can choose a practical—and ideally, simple—solution. For example, Billy took excellent care of Darlene when she was sick, but Darlene did not take care of Billy. When Billy told Darlene that this left him feeling neglected, she chose the following solution. First, she did something right away to nourish Billy. Although he wasn't currently ill, she could still help to restore the sense of well-being in the relationship by offering him some nurture. She made him some tea and rubbed his feet. Then she promised to make sure to nurture him next time he was sick. She kept her word. Three months later when Billy came down with the flu, Darlene nurtured him with a back rub, soup, her presence and assistance, washing the bed sheets and blanket, keeping the bedroom warm, driving him to a doctor, picking up herbs, teas, and medicines, reading stories to him, listening to him, and speaking lovingly and caringly to him. Darlene chose to give her best, and as a result her sense of well-being grew as much as Billy's from being attended to.

Well-Being Compatibility and Incompatibility

If you and a partner are compatible in the realm of well-being, your relationship will contribute to sensations that are warm and good. You will enjoy being with your mate because your body will feel better, your heart will feel better, and your mind will feel better quite a lot of the time when you are together.

If you are incompatible in this way, your body will feel worse, your head space will be worse, and your heart will not feel good when you are with each other.

As with all of the other areas, each individual can only be as happy with another as he or she is able to be with his or her self. Addressing your own contribution to your well-being is the place to start if things do not feel good. When you are caring well for yourself, you are in a better position to determine whether or not someone else is compatible with you in this area.

Relationships with and without Well-Being Compatibility

Partners who are incompatible in the area of well-being can experience exhaustion, disjointed feelings at home, and lack of nurture. Someone in this situation may find herself gravitating to other places and people to feel at home.

Partners who are compatible in the well-being realm feel good at home. Being together becomes a sweet haven where wellness can thrive. Compatible partners will go to each other and the life they share to rebuild strength, re-nourish, and replenish.

Well-being begins with the grace of emotional chemistry, grows with practical sense, and prospers with attentiveness. The apple grows juicy and full when the farmer tends to the land and the tree. Well-being is the same. Well-being is thought turned into action, communication expressed as service, and love turned into work. Lovers with compatible emotional chemistry need only tend to their well-being consciously to enjoy a life of rosy red cheeks like the apple in its prime.

Chapter 6
PASSION
sex in relationship

In the movies a lover's sunlit hair stays intact. She smiles happily, sighs softly, and her make-up never smears while making love. In the real bedroom, the candlelight softens the contours of her human face but you learn her true secrets. Her hair goes wild. Her back and hips dance. Her eyes shine while she screams, and in her scream joy, sorrow, and rage become one. Your lover's body sweats with desire. Passion is hot with fire in your heart, fluid like the river of life that runs through you, tingling all over your skin like a summer breeze, and settling you into your own muscles like the earth.

Passion is offered to you easily if you are a passionate person. You meet someone who sends you into ecstasy. Passion needs care to keep growing. Often it fades because we are unknowingly careless. Passion thrives in an environment of communication, appreciation, health, and ambient sensuality.

THE NECESSITY OF INNATE SEXUAL ATTRACTION

Passion is born of chemistry. If you meet the prince who easily becomes your best friend and fills your heart but doesn't fill your hips right now, chances are he won't in the future, either. Unfortunately, love does not guarantee passion. While the two become intimately connected in a healthy romantic relationship, they are born of separate homes. If you meet your princess, fall deep into love and lust, fulfill each other's wildest dreams for a couple of years, and two years later find that your passion has dwindled, you can get it back. If you meet your prince, fall into love and passion, and the love and passion continue year after year, you have much to be grateful for.

Keri and Casey met in math class in twelfth grade. They easily and effortlessly became best friends. They spent every afternoon together, every weekend together, and when they were apart they were often on the phone.

Keri loved to cuddle with Casey but never really enjoyed kissing. Casey loved to kiss Keri, so sometimes she went along with it and often she said no. Keri and Casey enjoyed touching each other's body. Casey wanted to feel himself inside of Keri but she said no.

Keri and Casey decided to go to the same college. After moving away from home Keri decided that she wanted to experience sexual intercourse. She didn't have a desire to feel Casey slip inside of her. She felt very turned on by a guy named Brad down the dorm hall. But Casey was her best friend and she loved him, so she assumed that the desire for him would grow if they had sex.

Casey had waited to have sex until Keri was ready, and it was his first time. He came very quickly. Keri didn't enjoy it. Ten years, two babies, seven sexuality workshops, fourteen books, and twenty-five counseling sessions later, Keri still didn't enjoy sex with her husband.

When Keri and Casey split up, Keri dated a man from work named Charlie. Her sex life was ecstatic, explosive, and everything she had longed for. Casey was heartbroken, but two years later he fell in love again and shared sexual fulfillment beyond his most delicious fantasies.

Passion requires sexual chemistry—innate desire from both partners toward the other. In the movies many a woman who falls into love naturally falls into lust. In the movies many a man who falls into lust naturally falls into love. In real life, of course, women and men can fall into love without falling into lust, can fall into lust without falling into love, or can fall into both. While the latter makes for a wonderfully delicious existence, the first two experiences can be disappointing. We can't fall in love or lust with someone just because we wish to. Neither one is a completely rational process. For this reason it is important that you feel a deep sexual desire for your partner.

Many couples who are compatible in every way but sexually end up at the therapist's office in hopes that their lack of passion is a psychological problem that can be changed. Almost all of the couples who come to therapy with this problem are aware of it because they have experienced profound passion in other relationships. When two people who have experienced passion in other loving relationships report that they have never experienced passion in a current relationship, I ask a lot of questions. I send them to a doctor to rule out organic causes, and I try to find out about their communication patterns to see if there are emotional and communication issues. Almost all of the time, couples who have had an experience of profound lust in other loving situations and have never experienced this with each other simply lack chemistry. No doctor or psychologist can change this. Some people can create lust by convincing themselves that it is there or deconditioning themselves from set ideas about who is attractive. Most, however, cannot create satisfying, authentic lust if the natural chemistry isn't present.

KEEPING PASSION ALIVE WITH VARIETY

Cindy and Jimmy lived in a shared aura of passion and delight from their first encounter. Their sex life was continuously fulfilling because it was consistently new. They learned new ways to touch, bought new scents, visited new environments, found new music, and tried new experiences regularly. As a result, their sex life was almost always fresh and fulfilling.

Rekindling Passion with Communication

Jack and Lydia were hot for each other for two years, but after the baby was born their sex life wilted. They were able to solve this dilemma by learning to talk about their many feelings openly and without blame. The constraints of a child in the house led to unanticipated disappointments and hardship, so by talking about their feelings and needs without reacting defensively, their romantic life was rekindled. By meeting their own needs they remained happier and had more to give to their daughter.

The Source of Individual Passion
Passion is the by-product of listening to your dreams and finding ways to bring them to life. Anyone who follows his or her visions and heart-callings experiences passion. Sex is an arena in which we can create a microcosm of our world with a partner through bodily expression.

PASSION COMPATIBILITY TEST
The following test will assist you in determining how compatible you are with your potential mate in the area of passion. Read each statement and choose the one that most closely represents you. Score your test on a continuum of **-1 to 2.**

2 The intensity of my passion with my partner is so strong that it overrides everything else. All I want to do with my partner is have sex.

1 I have always been attracted to my partner.

0 I am very attracted to my partner now.

-1 Sexual chemistry is missing.

Understanding Your Score
-1 You are with someone who is not compatible with you sexually. This will interfere with your passion. While you may experience profound passion as an individual in other areas of your life, the passion that lovers share will be blocked, causing an ongoing feeling of incompletion.

0-1 You have picked a great partner for you in the realm of passion.

2 You have picked an excellent partner for a temporary lover, but he or she is likely to disappoint you as a life mate.

HOW TO IMPROVE THE EXPRESSION OF PASSION

In order to improve the expression of passion, realize that sex is a story you write. You want to make it as pleasurable, nurturing, exciting, fun, authentic, and communicative as possible. Following are ways to improve your sex life in each of these categories.

Pleasure

Make sure that you fulfill all of your senses. Feast your eyes with a bedroom full of interior decorations that bring you delight. Visit places that keep you alert and looking around. Dress each other in clothes that you both find attractive and alluring.

Feed your ears with music. Make love to music that turns you on. Share your sighs. Bathe each other in warmly woven words of adoration.

Satisfy your nose with the air from outdoors, flowers, freshly cut grass, the ocean, or whatever it is that makes you want to feed yourself with deep breaths of air. Breath is the source of inspiration. Use oils, lotions, perfumes, and incense that you enjoy. The scent of sweat on a freshly bathed body is erotic as well.

Fill your mind with words. Speak to each other poetically. Compliment each other generously.

Feed your taste buds with kisses, sweets, and satiating meals before making love.

Nurture

Make sure that affection is part of your sex life. Massage each other. Cuddle. Hug. Play with different strokes, speeds, and types of touch. Touch vigorously, gently, smoothly, and with texture. Learn to know your partner through your body's intuition. Close your eyes and trust what you feel when you touch him. Then ask him how he likes to be touched and discover if your sense of him is accurate.

Excitement

Make sex exciting by sharing it in different places. You can find numerous places both inside and outside the house to be physically intimate: the walk-in closet, the ocean at night when the two of you are alone on the sand, the kitchen table, the hidden spot in the forest where nobody else has traveled. Try many different ways of making love. Be surprising and unexpected with what you say, what you do, where and how you initiate, and what you wear.

Fun

Sex is a time to play. Tell stories that make each other laugh. Look into each other's eyes. Roll around like kids. Find every way possible to adore each other.

Authenticity

Openly express what you feel, think, and desire in the moment. In the movies sex is only about sex and falling in love. In real life, sex is a multifaceted experience in which we share a variety of emotions, thoughts, and sensations. Share openly with your mate about what is really going on.

Connection

When you engage in all of the above interactions with your mate, your sex life will naturally feel connected. You will find closeness with each other.

Making Changes to Enhance Attraction

If your passion level toward your partner is fulfilling but some aspect of him or her is unattractive to you, it is fair to ask for a change. Improving our habit of adoring and complimenting each other is possible. Making it a point to be clean is an easy task. Choosing to wear scents and clothes that turn a partner on is an easy gift to give. Learning new ways of touching and sharing physical expression can be joyous. Changing interior decorations can be fun.

Choosing Someone Who Truly Delights You

Passion is not limited to your physical expression. It is important to pick a mate who delights you, leaves you tingling, and calls forth sensual celebration from your hips down into your roots and up into your tummy, your heart, your throat, your forehead, and your crown.

Your partner can turn you on with a glance, a word, a touch any time of the day. Passion is excitement we feel toward life independently. In a love relationship, one person's passion meets the other's. All kinds of things can ignite our passion for another: their way of communicating, their smell, their touch, their way of living, their way of thinking, their way of looking.

Passion is the energy of creation and generativity. This is not love. Love is the energy of the heart and can exist independently of passion. Passion and love combined create romantic love, which is completed in physical form. If you are not turned on to your partner's physical form, you are probably not with the right partner. If your partner's natural scent is unappealing to you, your passion is very likely to be squelched. Bodily passion is of a basic animal nature, which requires innate attraction.

Relationships with and without Passion Compatibility

Don't spend too much time on this one. Either you are both attracted to each other or you are not. I have seen clients who waited years for a platonic friendship to magically bloom into an ecstatic romance when it was not meant to be. The rationale for this is "I love him and he is my best friend so the passion will grow." This isn't necessarily so. In fact, while it does happen unexpectedly in some friendships, it is unlikely. If one or both of you doesn't feel a lot of attraction toward the other, don't fool yourself and think that you can grow some. It doesn't work that way.

If you think you have more passion for people you fantasize about, for imagined situations, specific body parts, or specific ways of expressing passion than for the discovery of sex with your partner, the problem is not compatibility. In this case you are having some intimacy and addiction conflicts that you will need to address individually, regardless of which partner you choose.

Couples who are compatible in the area of passion can always have that realm to return to for pleasure, closeness, and a feeling of being alive.

PASSION RISES IN YOUR HEART LIKE THE DAWN

Passion rises in your heart like the dawn, tingles in your belly like a warm meal, and spills out of your mind and into your body like spring rain. Passion is the dance of our animal roots, an enthusiasm that comes from deep within the body and soul, and a celebration of our existence. Choose a partner with whom passion comes alive, and your life will feel exciting and vibrant.

Chapter 7
PRACTICAL COMPATIBILITY
lifestyle in relationship

Practical compatibility, unlike the other six qualities discussed in this book, has no poetic description. This is because practical compatibility cannot be romanticized. It leaves no room for ambiguity. Practical compatibility is a must in a long-term relationship.   In order to live harmoniously and in a meaningful way as partners, two people must share common values and lifestyles. When people marry out of love or lust and have significantly different life plans, their relationship is either doomed or destined for great disappointment.

Marrying someone who is firmly grounded in a different religious, philosophical, or spiritual tradition, a distant geographic place, unfamiliar daily life, or who holds an incompatible future life plan, without first finding agreeable points of compromise, is like ordering a vanilla ice cream and then complaining because it isn't chocolate. It is important to have enough self-respect to marry someone who shares your values and lifestyle.

If you were in love in the middle of the ocean without a boat or life vest, and neither you nor your partner knew how to swim, would love save you? For how long?

Practical compatibility is a must in a lasting relationship. Without it you are on a road to disaster. Practical compatibility includes geographic location, religion and/or spirituality (or lack thereof), social life, family desires and values, leisure activities, and financial expectations.

Whereas grace requires surrender, practical compatibility requires will. How we choose to live is built upon how we utilize our will. Will is a very important part of being human. To live happily with someone our wills must be aligned in basic ways. If they are not, one person will try to change the other into something he or she isn't meant to be, and the result will be a power struggle with no end. For this reason it is necessary to choose a mate who has a life that is aligned with your own.

FINDING SHARED DESIRES AND ESTABLISHING COMPROMISE BEFORE MARRYING

Julia and Eliot married, then spent ten years arguing about where it would be best to raise children—in the suburbs or the country—but never came to an agreement. They then divorced with no children.

Miranda and Jacob married after agreeing to live in the city due to Miranda's desire and to vacation at a beach house all summer due to Jacob's desire. Jacob would have preferred to live in the country and Miranda would have preferred to go to Europe for a couple of weeks each summer, but both gave the other's desire precedence in one area and felt the joy of giving as well as receiving. Both were happy with the marriage.

Shawn and Charlie were both excited about buying a home by the bay and shared enjoyment in doing so. Their path offered rewards with ease. Mutual compromise or shared lifestyle expectations are necessary when making a commitment.

PRACTICALITY COMPATIBILITY TEST

The following test will help you determine if you and your mate are practically compatible. If the answer to any of these questions is true for one of you but false for the other, mark the answer as false. Score your test on a continuum of 17 to 36.

Children

My mate and I both want children, or neither of us want children.

1 true

2 false

Bringing Up Children (only for those who desire children)

My mate and I have many compatible views regarding children. Areas in which we differ are negotiable.

1 true

2 false

Religion/Spirituality

My mate and I share religion or spirituality or atheism in a way that is at least satisfactory for us both. If compromise is needed, we have arrived at compromises that are satisfactory to us both.

1 true

2 false

Geographic Location

My mate and I desire to live in the same area or have arrived at a compromise that is at least satisfactory to us both.

1 true

2 false

Daily Schedule

I am satisfied with the amount of time my mate and I spend together given our daily schedules, or we have agreed to co-create a mutually satisfying schedule.

1 true

2 false

Weekends

My mate and I plan weekends in a way that feels good to me, or we have agreed to do so in the future with a realistic plan.

1 true

2 false

Vacations

My mate and I enjoy vacations together because our desires are similar enough.

1 true

2 false

Pets

My mate and I have come to a satisfactory agreement regarding living with or not living with pets.

1 true
2 false

Eating

My mate and I enjoy eating together.

1 true
2 false

Substances

My mate and I are satisfied with each other's relationship to substances. (For example, both agree that there is no smoking in the house.)

1 true
2 false

Friends

My mate and I are satisfied with the level of interest each shows in the other's friends.

1 true
2 false

Family

My mate and I are satisfied with the level of involvement we maintain with each other's family.

1 true
2 false

Music, TV

My mate and I enjoy similar music and TV, or feel okay about hearing each other's music and TV shows in the house.

1 true
2 false

Interior Decorations

My mate and I are able to decorate the home together in a way that is pleasing to us both.

1 true
2 false

Cleanliness

My mate and I are satisfied with each other's cleaning standards and habits.

1 true
2 false
Money
My mate and I are satisfied with each other's financial contribution to the household.
1 true
2 false
Health
My mate and I are satisfied with each other's health standards and practices.
1 true
2 false

Understanding Your Score
17
You have the foundation for pleasure and ease.
18-36
You must arrive at a satisfying compromise to any questions that were answered "false." The compromise can be mutual or within yourself.   Otherwise, end the relationship. A relationship with practical incompatibility dooms the two people to unhappiness.

A MODERN TRAGIC FABLE
David climbed the steps to the diving board, knowing all along that the pool was empty. But the pool was in the back of the honeymoon resort hotel. Resort hotels don't have empty pools. David thought that he was seeing things. The pool had to be full! How could it be empty? It was spring. It was a resort for lovers. The birds were chirping. The sun was bright and Dave was in love. It's my bad eyesight, David thought.
David smashed his head and ended his life because he was unwilling to trust what he saw. Love was supposed to conquer all. Without practical compatibility, love does

conquer all. Do you want to be conquered or do you want to be happy?

What to Expect with and without Practical Compatibility

Couples that do not share practical compatibility will suffer from feeling alone, disappointed, frustrated, and neglected on a regular basis. Love will not make up for this. One man, Karl, chose to be with a woman he loved deeply and even proposed to despite the lack of practical compatibility in their relationship. He was willing to feel isolated and alone a lot of the time because he felt warm and close to her.

His girlfriend, Susan, realized soon after he proposed that she would never be happy enough. She began to date only men who shared her lifestyle in many important ways. After a few disappointing relationships with practically compatible partners with whom love was not as strong as it had been with Karl, she began to wonder. Did she make a mistake? Did she slap love in the face? Had she asked too much of life?

She didn't give up her desire for a mate despite her despondent thoughts.

The next time she fell in love she fell more deeply in love than ever. She was delighted because for the first time in her life she was in love with someone who also shared her lifestyle. As a result, love was easy instead of a struggle. Her current partner, Alex, shares deeper communication, connection, and intimacy with her. She is very happy that she did not marry Karl, and that she waited for someone who could meet her on all important levels.

Karl, on the other hand, fell in love with Joyce. Joyce's lifestyle had many similarities to Susan's. He proposed and Joyce said yes. Now he is married. Both he and Joyce feel deeply in love but experience ongoing dissatisfaction with each other's different lifestyle desires. Karl says that's the way his relationships are. You make the choice about your own.

Practical Lifestyle Compatibility and Incompatibility

Couples whose lifestyles are compatible in the ways most important to them report a sense of ease with living day-to-day life and making plans. Couples who are incompatible in this area find themselves to be in frequent states of disappointment and unpleasant surprise.

When grace, perspective, communication, love, emotional chemistry, or passion are strong, it is tempting to overlook practical incompatibility. As the honeymoon period wears off, however, practical incompatibility becomes increasingly uncomfortable. By giving yourself the time to agree upon compromises and make peace with them, you set yourself up for a lasting lantern light when the road is dark. By choosing a mate who walks on the same road as you, you can leave the lantern at home. You will walk in the sun.

Chapter 8
Conclusion
The overall relationship in balance

Compatibility Signs
Crown Chakra: Grace

People who are compatible in grace will have a sense of grace within their individual lives. Together they will experience trust in love and self. People who are not compatible will find that the relationship encourages a loss of trust in life and self.

Third Eye Chakra: Wisdom

People who are compatible with wisdom will both have a positive attitude. Together they will remain engaged, interested, and stimulated. People who are not compatible in the area of wisdom will experience profound loneliness.

Throat Chakra: Communication

People who are compatible in communication will both have a style of no-blame, respectful, self-responsible, expressive communication. Together they will find workability. People who are not compatible in this area will encounter repeated conflict.

Solar Plexus Chakra: Power

People who are compatible in this area will both have a strong sense of self-worth and boundaries. Together they will share warmth and happiness. People who are not compatible in this area will feel somewhat at a loss or will engage in power struggles.

Sex Chakra: Passion and Generation

People who are compatible in this area will both be familiar with ongoing passion in their lives. Together they will feel sexual fulfillment. People who are not compatible will feel unfed longing.

Root Chakra: Practical Life

People who are compatible in practical life will both have had a working, functional life as individuals before they met. They will find ease in living with their partner. People who are not matched in this area of life will experience frustration and repeated disappointment.

It is mandatory that you clarify your needs in a relationship. If you are unclear about your needs, you are likely to choose an unsatisfying relationship. Many people waste years of precious time trying to change a partner or forcing themselves to be happy in situations that go against their basic nature or desires.

Many great Saints and teachers have removed themselves from the world of distractions to become unconditionally loving. In the same way, remove yourself from partnership that is destined for extra hardship due to incompatibility. There is no need to use a relationship as a great challenge. A wonderful relationship will provide enough challenge for you to become a better person. Choose one that is easy and effortless in all of the major areas so that you can be the love you desire, experience the joy you desire, and turn living into a delightful event.

Once you choose to be with someone who meets your basic criteria, you will still encounter opportunities for growth. Life will always be full of imperfections and disappointments. It is necessary to live with these, maintaining a flexible stance, and to stay primarily focused on the gifts that life brings. When you treat yourself to choosing a mate who meets your most important requirements, it will be easier to remain in a state of gratitude. Adjustments will take place with a lot less effort and resistance when you are generally satisfied.

Sometimes life presents us with a situation that forces us to reexamine what it is that we think we need. For example, when Leslie asked Rich to move to the city with her, he said absolutely not. Eight months after parting ways, both Leslie and Rich missed each other deeply. Richard reexamined his need to live in the suburbs and realized that the issue for him wasn't suburbs vs. city but rather a feeling of safety vs. a feeling of stress. Richard decided it was worth his time to try living in the city. He moved to the city to be with Leslie open-heartedly and found to his surprise that he was happier than ever. The new friends he made and experiences he had gave him a kind of joy he hadn't known since childhood. Unexpectedly for him, he felt safer and less stressed than he had in years. His faith in life deepened, and he became a person who felt safer within himself. Making a compromise turned out to be a gift that provided him with what he most sought.

Jeremy, on the other hand, moved from California to Florida with his wife, Sharman, because she wanted to be near her family. He didn't want to go but agreed. He moved with resentment and a closed heart and was miserable. Sharman felt depressed living with a miserable husband. Jeremy made a compromise in action but not with any attempt to find his own happiness. He simply did what his wife asked. Making a compromise with this kind of attitude will bring toxicity to a relationship.

Compromise can be wonderful or dreadful, depending on attitude. It is important to never make a compromise unless you do so selfishly. When you serve another in order to serve yourself you will know happiness. When you serve another at the expense of yourself you will know unhappiness.

It is also important when you share your life with someone that it be a person who can meet you in the ways that are of most importance to you. Before making a life-long commitment, make sure that your mate meets any requirements you have in the areas of grace, wisdom, communication, love, well-being, passion, and practical compatibility. The details can always be changed. When basic desires are met, compromises and adjustments will feel worthwhile.

Grace flies above you, yet lands in your garden. Wisdom explains to you what grace is doing when she fails to glide, falls into form, and eats your roses. Communication keeps you close when wisdom is shared. Love fills your heart when communication keeps you close. Well-being offers a container on Earth for profound and amorphous love. Passion keeps you tied together in a dance of well-being. Practical compatibility allows grace, wisdom, communication, love, well-being, and passion to stay alive year after year.

The seven significant categories in mate choice carry the meaning of the seven chakras: crown, third eye, throat, heart, solar plexus, genital, and root. Honor the basic aspects of life that have been bestowed upon you by life itself. Take care of yourself, and you will be taken care of by life.

Sessions for individuals and couples

www.counselingscottsvalley.us

www.DrLaurieMoore.com

831-477-700

Laurie@DrLaurieMoore.com

Readings for Individuals and Couples

www.animiracles.com